Just Take You

BARBARA BELL

Just Take Your Frock Off

A LESBIAN LIFE

Edited by
Brighton Ourstory Project

OURSTORY BOOKS
BRIGHTON

First published in Great Britain in 1999 by
Ourstory Books
PO Box 2861, Brighton BN1 1UN

Copyright © 1999 Barbara Bell and Ourstory Ltd

The right of Ourstory Ltd to be identified as the author of this work
has been asserted in accordance with the Copyright, Designs and
Patents Act 1988

British Library Cataloguing in Publication Data
A catalogue record of this book is available from the British Library

ISBN 0 9535880 0 9

Lines on page 47 from 'I'll See You Again' reproduced by permission
of International Music Publications Ltd. Words by Noël Coward
© 1929 Chappell Music Limited. Warner/Chappell Music Limited,
London W6 8BS.

Bitter Sweet programme on page 39 reproduced by permission of
Manchester Central Library, Arts Library Theatre Collection.

The publishers gratefully acknowledge the following for allowing their
pictures to be reproduced in this book: Tracie Hammond, page 174;
Popperfoto, pages 63 and 78. The pictures on pages 35, 50, 69 and
148 are from the Brighton Ourstory Project collection, and all other
pictures are from Barbara Bell's personal and family collections.

Designed and typeset by Joyce Chester.

Back cover colour photo by Lynne Fox.

Printed and bound in Great Britain by Delta Press, Hove.

Contents

Introduction

Just Take Your Frock Off was assembled by Brighton Ourstory Project from over forty hours of taped conversations with Barbara Bell. Working with Barbara was a joy. To our knowledge, this is the first time in Britain that a lesbian of Barbara's generation has given a full and explicit account of her own life. We have done our best to protect the privacy of other individuals, which has unfortunately meant that we were unable to use certain photographs of Barbara with her friends.

Brighton Ourstory Project is a lesbian and gay history group, which was established in 1989. We also produced the much-acclaimed book, *Daring Hearts, Lesbian and Gay Lives of 50s and 60s Brighton*.

Linda Pointing and Tom Sargant
Brighton Ourstory Project
May 1999

Barbara Bell and Brighton Ourstory Project would like to thank the following for their help:
Aïne, Alistair, Allie Rogers, Andrew Kay, Andrew Le Flohic, Bob Dobson, Charles Drazin, Chris Adams, Chris Farrah-Mills, Dani Ahrens, Emma, Emma Donoghue, Sir Harry Hinsley, Jacky Bratton, Jane Traies, Jean Wooller, Jenny Bennett, Jill Gardiner, Joyce Chester, Lynne Fox, Madeleine, Margaret Monod, Marian Devoy, Midge Smith, Monica at the Only Alternative Left, Moss Allison,

Pat McCulloch, Peter Allinson, Peter Dennis, Rose Collis, Sheila, Siobán Clark, Stephanie Davis, Thomas Tunnock, Tracie Hammond, Bentley Motor Museum, Blackburn Reference Library, Bletchley Park Trust, Brighton & Hove Resource Centre, Brighton & Hove Lesbian & Gay Resource Centre, Brighton Women's Walking Group, Crawley Reference Library, EMI Archive, Fawcett Library, London Guildhall University, Foreign & Commonwealth Office Library, Hove Citizens Advice Bureau, Imperial War Museum, Kensington Central Reference Library, Manchester Central Library (Arts and Local Studies Departments), Metropolitan Women Police Association, Police Museum, Sussex Aids Centre & Helpline, City of Westminster Archive.

I had a wonderful dream, I had it for years, I'm so sorry it stopped. It was always in Brighton station, I could show you the spot. I would start jumping a little bit and people would stop when they were passing and think, Oh, what's she doing? Every time I jumped I went a bit higher. I had to hold my breath and that made me lighter and I went higher and higher until I got to the roof and my head would rest gently on the glass. By then everybody had stopped and everybody was watching and sometimes people would shout, "Come down! Come down!" – thought I was going to fall. I'd stay up there as long as I fancied and then glide down again. It was a wonderful feeling going up on the air under your own steam as high as you wanted.

1

A Simple Uncluttered Life

I'm so grateful I was never captured into marriage. Even today people who don't know my background, ignorant people, think I've not married because I've been shoved aside, had some misfortune. Misfortune! I'm very lucky to be a lesbian. I never wished to be anything else. I should think I'm the oldest lesbian in Brighton, or at least the longest active lesbian. I've been a lesbian for seventy years now.

I was born in Blackburn, Lancashire on the 13th of December, 1914. My mother always told everybody that was her lucky number, thirteen. When I was quite tiny I had meningitis and the doctor said, "I don't think she's going to live and if she does I can't be sure she won't have brain damage. It's really in the hands of God, there's nothing more I can do." They were in despair. Grandma Stankley was in doing her bit of nursing, and my mother made the suggestion that perhaps they should go to the Mission. The Saturday night church concert was on. My mother went and whispered to the vicar and the concert stopped. He announced that Mr and Mrs Bell's baby was seriously ill and not expected to survive the night – would they all please get on their knees and he would conduct a prayer.

Back they went home and Grandma Stankley said, "I think she's passed the crisis. She's been sweating buckets, I've been mopping her forehead and she's sleeping now." My mother and father swore it was a direct answer to prayer. When the doctor came Sunday morning, he couldn't believe that I had turned the corner so quickly and was sure I was going to get well without brain damage. My dad used to joke about that afterwards and say, "Oh well, it's when she had that sickness, it left her brain a bit touched."

Grandma Stankley was not a grandma of ours, she was just a grandma of everybody's in the street. She was a spinster and didn't seem to have any family. She was a wise old woman, always there if there was a crisis. If there was a baby born, run for Grandma Stankley. She would know what to do, help the midwife. If somebody died, she knew how to wash the body, put pennies on the eyes. If Baby was having a fit, run for Grandma Stankley. Babies always seemed to be having fits in those days.

My mam and my dad were both from really humble backgrounds. My father worked in the cotton mill. He was an overlooker, what was called a tackler. They used to make jokes about them – tackler jokes like Irish jokes. He was a good-looking fella and very romantic, used to write poems to my mother and bring her flowers which was unusual for a factory man. They were very musical. My father had a beautiful tenor voice and he sang in the St Cecilia Choir in Blackburn. I remember my mother playing her mandolin and my father singing when I was little. It was such a simple uncluttered life. It was very happy. I had a good foundation. What I am today is what my parents made me.

My sister Midge is ten years younger than me. We had a brother, Stanley, who was killed in the Second World War. We lived in Johnston Street which was off the Preston New Road. As you went downhill from the Preston New Road, the slummier it got. The houses got smaller and scruffier and they were all back-to-backs in long rows. They were the poorest class with the cheapest rents and the most children – the ones that looked ragged. And if you went uphill from the Preston New Road, that was the big houses and the park. My mother used to tell me that if you looked in their dustbins, you would find more jam jars than anywhere in the poor district because they always had jam for tea. It was all a bit of a swank, she said. Well, we lived down the hill but before you got to the lower strata. We were the dividing line. My dad always used to say,

Family picnic c. 1926, Barbara far left.

•

"You're working-class and proud of it." We were the hard-working, ordinary people. Although we had no high falutin ideas, my father always wanted me to better myself, as he called it. If I made friends, they had to be friends that lived in the next street higher than we did.

Our house wasn't a back-to-back. It was a bit superior because we had a little alleyway running between us. They were owned by the town, beautiful little houses. We made them beautiful – palaces.

We're proud people in Lancashire, very proud people. Friday night was doing your front. Everybody in the street would be out with a long broom and a bucket of soda water scrubbing the flags and the doorstep. It dried white and then you'd come out with a clean bucket of water, wash it all down and it used to come up lovely. Then the fella would come along with his little cart shouting, "Rags! Rags! Rags!" and you'd run out with any old rags and he'd give you a donkey stone. It was like compressed chalk. You would dip this stone into some water and rub it all over the step and underneath the window where it was stonework. You'd wipe it very smooth with your cloth so you wouldn't see any streaks. It was just like it had been painted – it was beautiful. If you had yellow stone, you usually had yellow lace curtains – you could have yellow, cream or white.

The brickwork was red – you never touched that – you'd go over it if it got dusty with your dry brush. When they'd proudly done all this, you'd see them standing, leaning against the doorjamb with their arms folded and their aprons on, looking at their work and saying, "Yes, it looks lovely, doesn't it?" If it was raining they'd bring the aspidistra out and put it on the pavement to give it a wash.

Round the back was the petty – never called the lavatory. It was right at the bottom of the yard with a wooden seat and all the muck used to go in a tub. Once a week the pettyman would come up the back a cart and empty the damn thing. Your mother would scrub the seat, a real beautiful white board. Some people had a double one, two seats, and you used to sit there with your pal. If you were going to be a long time, you'd take some newspaper with you and tear it up and thread it with a skewer – put string through and hang it behind the door for toilet paper.

If you were fortunate, you had a tiny strip about a foot wide the length of the wall to have a bit of garden. They were very tall walls, you couldn't peep over unless somebody poked you up. And on the wall you had the bath hanging, the big zinc bath, about five feet long. It used to be brought in on bath night, every Friday. Cleanest in first, dirtiest in last. If it was cold, we would have a big fire. It was lovely being bathed in front of a coal fire then being rubbed down with a towel.

We all had our duties around the house. Windows were part of my duty, Saturday mornings, all the windows. Water and a bit of vinegar and a wash leather, none of this easy spray stuff that you've got now. I hated it so I'd bribe my grandpa with ginger biscuits and he'd do the windows for me.

My mother ran the house. My father was the man of the house but she had a pretty good say in what happened, in an unobtrusive way. She held the purse strings. My father would come home from work and put his wages on the table. He'd have his pot of tea and his newspaper handed to him. He'd be given enough for a haircut and my mam would keep the rest to save for holidays and pay for the bills and the food and the clothes. What a mam she was. She seemed to know everything about everything – without being taught or told. She was the essence of the family somehow. In my pea-brain she almost had an aura round her. She was like an angel to me.

My father would play with us after tea. He used to play till my mother had to say, "Stop Joe, stop, it's going to end in tears." We had a big square table. One of my favourite games was to sit on this table, my dad got underneath on all fours and he'd lift it up with his back and shake it about. I'd scream with joy. Even when I was quite big, I loved this game. Invariably I fell off and there were tears but it didn't matter, it was worth it.

My dad used to say, "Come here, I want to speak to you," and he'd sit me on his knee and he'd say, "Now, I've something to ask you and I want a decent answer. I want you to tell me truthfully, who do you love best, your mam or me?" It was always the same answer. I'd whisper, "Both the same." And he'd roar with laughter and clap his hands.

My dad was marvellous but he was a strict disciplinarian. He was Victorian. In those days if you were a good father you slapped your children when they were naughty. If we'd done something very, very wrong, he had a strap hanging up in the kitchen to sharpen his razor on, he'd cut tails in the bottom of it and you'd get it on your legs or on your bum. It never made marks but it was, I remember, damn humiliating.

Naughty usually meant answering back or disobedience or if you told a lie – that was terrible. You didn't tell the same lie twice. A smack on the face if you were saying something bad with your mouth. Or a smack on the legs if you'd done something that involved legs. I used to think it was fair if I'd done wrong.

When my grandma died we moved into the family house so that my mother could look after her widowed father and her brother, the lovely Uncle Jack who had never left home. It was a large house and we had a bathroom which was a great luxury. My mother had the idea that it would be nice to have a pink bath. She'd read about some paint you could use. We had to wait a long time for the paint to get really hard. Then my father took the first bath. We were downstairs and we heard him shouting, "Bea! Beatrice! Help!" His bottom was stuck to the bath. We stood round the door laughing until my mam shooed us away. I don't know how she got him out in the end. Men cry and shout for nothing. If they prick their finger there's a hoo-ha.

Our Uncle Jack doted on us. He belonged to the Magic Circle and he used to go round conjuring at children's parties. Then he had a cinematograph show and we used to bring all our pals in whilst he showed Charlie Chaplin films. Because he was a single man he had the money to do these things – he was the manager of a big glaziers.

He had a boyfriend called Victor. Victor was very dark. He had a little tash and he'd beautiful black shiny hair. He was a little bit shorter than my Uncle Jack and a bit stubbier. They used to do everything together, go off for holidays, they were great pals.

Even then I thought it was a bit odd. Later my friend Cyril said, "Oh yes, they're at it." But they never flaunted it and waved their arms about – they were men. Victor lived only a few streets away with his mother so he often came to our house, he was accepted as one of the family. I grew up with them both. I don't ever remember Jack not being with Victor. And in fact my brother was called after him – Stanley Victor.

My uncle was just wonderful with children but he was well past the normal marrying age. And then he met a woman at church and got engaged to her. Victor went mad, he actually went crazy and I remember them taking him off to hospital, saying that he'd gone crazy in the head. Very soon after that he died. Whether he had committed suicide we were never told, never went to the funeral or anything. My mother told us we had to be very understanding with my Uncle Jack because Victor was his best friend.

Jack did get married in the end. They adopted a child who turned out to have some weird disease that nobody could cure. He died at the age of eleven after being hawked all round the hospitals. My uncle would have made a smashing dad because he loved children. His wife was a funny woman and nobody much took to her.

2

Angels Round Our Sofa

Maggie Smith was my great buddy when we were small. My mother was wont to go to the market on Wednesdays. Often she would call on her way back and pick me up from school. On one occasion she was going late to the market so she said, "Bring Maggie Smith in with you, I'll leave you a bit of tea and you can have tea together."

We hadn't been in long. It was a lovely warm day. In the living room we had lace curtains. They looped to the side and it was a great art getting these loops exactly right so you could see the neighbours but not too much. I pulled the curtains to and said, "Let's take our clothes off." She said, "What for?" I said, "Well, it's a hot day, just take your frock off, let's just dance about." She was a bit shy. I think that's why I liked her, because I could lead and she would always follow.

So we were getting our clothes off. We hadn't a stitch on. We didn't do anything. We didn't cuddle each other or fondle each other. Just danced around happy without clothes on. I remember the feeling to this day. It was sheer devilment. Then I looked at the clock, I said, "Oh, I think we'd better be getting dressed, me mother'll be coming back." So we got dressed and of course, it was hell to get the curtains back into these nice loops. We did our best with them, we thought they looked all right. First words when my mother came in: "What've you been doing with the curtains?" I said, "Oh, well, we sort of let them down, we didn't want people..."

"What were you doing that you didn't want people to see? What were you up to?"

Then of course it came out. My mother thought it was dreadful.

I suppose she thought we'd been at something. So we got a bit of a chiding and Maggie Smith was barred from the home for two weeks.

Girls were always given dolls. I never went overboard on them. I did like going to the dolls' hospital where they had rows of pot heads, all staring down at you. I remember my very first doll – I was very young – I went up to my grandma's on Christmas morning to show her. I was walking backwards and gazing around and I turned and hit a lamppost and smashed the doll's head. I screamed and ran home. Grandma never saw it with its head on.

Life was far too interesting to play with dolls. Summer, you got a length of prickly rope from the greengrocer, it came round the orange boxes. You could throw it over the lamppost arm and make a knot and you'd sit in it and wind yourself round the lamppost. You'd let go and fly back and unwind at great speed all through the summer nights. It was wonderful. But you had to look out for Larry the lamplighter because sometimes the gas mantle would get broken with you all kicking the lamppost to get yourself a bit wider out.

We had buck-and-stick and hopscotch on the pavement and we played at shops. We'd grind up different colours of stone for different ingredients, we'd get little tin lids or old bottles and we used to make super, super shops and go shopping.

We weren't far off what we called The Fields, where there were a few huts and chickens and allotments. You'd take a long broom handle and a big sheet and peg yourself out a little tent and go in there with your Spanish juice. You'd been to the chemist and bought a very hard piece of black liquorice and you'd chopped it up and put it in a medicine bottle and put it in a dark place. That was Spanish juice. If you shook it a long time, you got a froth on top. Suck off all the froth and then everybody else would have a suck. Used to play doctors and nurses and teachers. I was always a bossy teacher, one to be the leader.

On Sundays you went to church in the morning then you went

to Sunday school in the afternoon then church in the evening again. When the church was over you went down to the marketplace where there'd be people standing on soapboxes and praising the Lord. They'd say, "Now put your hand up if you want to be saved." I can't think how many times I was saved. Then we'd all chant and sing: "I'm S-A-V-E-D, I'm S-A-V-E-D." You just went for the sheer pleasure of making a big noise echoing round the marketplace.

We joined the Band of Hope in the local school. We all swore to abstain from drink and signed the temperance pledge. They used to show slides and talk, showing you a drunken father coming home and how bad it would be for the children, what a naughty man he was. My father wasn't a drinking man, never went to the pubs or anything like. The only wine we ever had in our house was the blackberry wine my mother made.

Late May was Whitsuntide — Whit Saturday, Whit Sunday and Whit Monday — and all the factories closed, everything shut down. Every church had its banner, an enormous thing that strong young men had to carry. If you were very honoured and you were little enough, you were allowed to walk under the banner with a basket of flowers or a wreath round your head. We walked in a great long procession, all through the town, into the country.

We used to get a jam bun and a currant bun in a paper bag and then you went with your mug to the beer barrel but instead of beer coming out, it was hot coffee. It was a great festival and there was always a brass band playing. We danced about doing little country dances and perhaps a few ball games or racing games and then when it was getting midgy and a bit cold, sun going in, you'd all troop back home. Every family went and if you were at loggerheads with your neighbours, you buried it all. Everybody was friends at Whitsuntide.

When I was eight I went into the big school and by God they gave you a good training there. I remember learning parts of the

Whitsuntide, Blackburn.

•

Bible and the Prayer Book and parts of history and chunks of poetry, Tennyson, Blake, Shakespeare, and your times tables and your verbs. That was the ritual every morning first thing. I can tell you all the books of the Bible, the Ten Commandments, I had to learn every one of those off by heart and the Creed and certain psalms. Even if I didn't know what they meant I loved chanting them, and singing, "Let the angels round our sofa..." I thought, why should they come round our sofa? It was 'the angels round us hover' but for years I thought it was round our sofa. I just sang it lustily and enjoyed the singing of it. Nice to think the angels were round our sofa.

One time the teacher was called out for something and whilst we were reciting our um-de-da-um-de-da, one of the little boys went off to the front and undid his trousers and started walking around waving his willy about everywhere. The boys were falling about laughing and the girls were covering their faces or having a quick look. When the teacher came back, we were still falling about and he got found out – three strokes of the cane on his hand.

We got hit for anything really – answering the teacher back or fighting in the playground or writing on the wall with a bit of chalk or going out of the school gates without your hat on. The slipper was better than the cane, didn't hurt so much, hit you on the bum with a plimsoll they kept specially for the purpose.

We used to have wonderful playground games amongst ourselves. Marbles, chequers, whip and top. Big Ship Sail Through the Alley-alley-oh and Chase and really organised games you sang to. Boys would have their games, we would have our games. There was a beautiful occupation called Peeps. Two of us would put on a peepshow in the lavatories and the other girls would have to pay a forfeit to come in and look – a couple of sweets or a lick of their cocoa and sugar that they'd brought in a little screw of paper. One of us would sit on the seat and one would stand behind the door in some posing position like statues. You opened the door and let them peep and then shut the door. It was never anything rude. You might be sitting on the seat with your arms round each other pretending to be lovers but never vulgar. You had your clothes on. You might put your blouse on back to front so you looked a bit different and bring a hat so one could look like a man.

We all had a nickname or rhyme and little gangs. Two or three of the boys thought it was a big laugh to sing:

> Barbara Bell went to hell
> To stitch the Devil's breeches.
> The Devil said to Barbara Bell
> "Don't make such damn big stitches."

They said damn, that was a big thing if children ever said damn.

We always had a proper breakfast. We didn't get anything at school. Nothing at all. The poor ones used to get cod liver oil. If they fainted in assembly because they hadn't had any breakfast, they were revived with a hot drink. There were quite a few poor families. When the parents were out of work and it was a lean year, they couldn't feed their children properly.

When you got home from school, if you were lucky you got a butty with sugar or a layer of jam. And then you'd have your high tea. You never sat round the fire with it on a plate, you sat at the table properly. We'd have Scotch broth or hot cockles and mussels tipped in a great big dish in the middle of the table. Then we'd have a hot milk drink before we went to bed. You were never denied bread – bread and jam – but usually you were content just to have a drink. My mother must have been a very thrifty woman because we went all through the Depression and we were never hungry.

Visiting the mill to see my dad was rather an adventure. Children weren't allowed in, really. You'd to stand at the swing doors and wait for the machinery to stop before you could go in. The young lads would come in then, to go underneath the looms and sweep up the dust from the cotton. The machinery was so noisy the weavers couldn't speak but some of them learned to lip-read. They had to concentrate because if a thread broke they had to damn well get it threaded up again straight away or else the machines would stop and then they'd to get the overlooker – that was my dad, Joe Bell.

There was a knocker-upper employed by the mill. He had a long pole with a wire brush on the end and in the mornings he would scratch your bedroom window to wake you up. He'd go all the way up the street because nearly everybody went to the mill. After he'd passed there'd be silence and then the sound of the clogs would start, bmm, bmm, like an army. The women in the winter time would be wrapped in their patterned shawls, hurrying to the mill.

It was never expected that I would go into the mill. No, I was Joe Bell's girl. His children hadn't to be slaves in the mines or the spinning and weaving factories. It was honourable work but he wanted life to be easier for us and more prosperous. Education was the passport to a job outside the mill. My mam and my dad sent for books from John Bull – Dickens, Scott, Dumas, Shakespeare. Working-class people used to read a lot in those days and were often very knowledgeable like my parents. They were keen on me getting the best education I could.

My father was working all the time until the slump when the factories began to close down. Then he was out of work. During the General Strike, particularly in the North, things were very tight. And many people were unemployed because India and other places out East had taken our market for cotton goods. We were poor. We'd go with a pram along the railway line, picking up pieces of coal to take home to make a fire, coal that had fallen off the trucks. Everybody was poor. If you had some food and you knew somebody was ill you shared it. Many and many an errand I was sent on with a pan of broth or pigeon soup, which was supposed to be nourishing.

People cared. It was all very friendly and neighbourly. I'm not saying there weren't bad times and bad people. You'd see drunks sometimes or some crazy woman clinging to a lamppost. We had a crazy woman relative came from Canada to see my father. I think her husband paid for her to come hoping she'd never return. Today she'd be having treatment. She used to cling to the lamp and sing when it was dark. I remember all the relatives clubbing together to send her back.

We didn't grumble. Nobody grumbled. The brass bands still played and we had the countryside, that was free. You could still afford a tram ride that took you out the town.

But my Dad, he hated being in the dole queue. He was not going to stand at the dole for thirty-two shillings a week when he was an honest working man. He just couldn't stomach it. He got a job as a milkman which was about five shillings more. But he had to work hard to get that. They were doing a lot of building on the outskirts of the town and a new housing estate didn't have any delivery of milk at all. If my father could get enough promises from people who were moving in, enough to make a round, they would give him a cart and he could have a job. He spent hours and he worked up a round. Winter time when it was raining, my sister Midge used to go to certain points on his round with a change of clothes under a big mac for him because he'd be soaked. He wasn't covered, it was an open cart with a horse. We used to be always drying clothes round the fire in the wintertime when it was rainy weather.

3

Really Forceful Crushes

When I was eleven I went to the Church of England Central School for Girls. It was actually in the churchyard of the cathedral and we would run round the gravestones playing tig. Once I had a shilling between my teeth for the cookery lesson and somebody hit me and this shilling shot down my throat. So the teachers were turning me upside down and banging me on the back. I was gasping away and they took me over to the cookery room and gave me bread to make this shilling go down. I was saying, "It's here, it's here," tapping my chest. Finally they thought they'd better take me off to hospital.

Miss Dent, my favourite teacher, offered to take me, so it was worth having a shilling down my throat. This was a real crush. I did have really forceful crushes. I was always looking at the other girls and the teachers. I wouldn't have minded if I'd swallowed an elephant – I was going in the car with Miss Dent.

The nurse tried to take it out with what they called a coin catcher. It was just a tube with a little pincer on the end. Well, since I couldn't swallow a little tiny lung healer that was the size of a pin head, could I swallow this thing? I was screaming my head off and kicking so they said, "Oh well, we'll put her to sleep." Next thing I knew I was coming round and there the shilling was on the bedside table. When I got home some of the class bought me a big bunch of grapes. We never had grapes in our family. I really enjoyed ill health for a few days.

I don't think I was a tomboy particularly but we used to have pranks. I used to walk home with two or three girls and we would play Nick-Nack. Took it in turns to knock on a particular door

Geography lesson c. 1926, Barbara front row, second from right.

•

before pelting off down the street. One day going back to school, there was a woman I'd never seen in my life standing at the school-gates with a teacher, saying, "That's one, that's one, yes, she's one." This woman's husband was ill upstairs in the house and of course she'd had to come down the stairs each time because it might have been something important.

The headmistress had us in and she said, "It's Friday, I can't deal with you now. I'll think what I'll do with you on Monday morning. I should think you'll all have to be expelled. I'm not having this sort of girl in my school." It was a hell of a weekend. I didn't dare tell my parents. It was considered very dreadful. And when we had this Monday morning reckoning, we had to stand in front of the school and standing behind us were all the staff. Everybody could see us because we were going to be told what a terrible thing we had done. I stood in front of Miss Dent. A couple started blubbing and she poked me in the back with her finger. She said, "Don't you dare cry." So I didn't dare cry, even if I'd wanted to.

She was very tough, a real disciplinarian. In nature study you had to draw a bluebell if it was bluebell time and name the parts. If your pencil wasn't sharp she would say, "Let me see that pencil!" and she'd stab you in the back of the hand with it.

I left at fourteen so I didn't get much schooling. I remember most of the things they taught me but I hated it on the whole. I was never at the top of the class, even at the prospect of having a bicycle if I got in the top ten. I was always halfway down the list. Perhaps I was a late developer because when I went to evening class I romped ahead. I didn't like to be treated as a child, as a schoolgirl. I didn't like it a bit.

It was around then that I first decided I wanted a flat in London. Everyone was saying, "Oh, I want to get married, I want to live in the country." They all wanted a cottage with roses round the door. What a thing to want! I'd just say, "Oh no, I want a flat in London. It's got to be in London. It's got to be a flat." It was modern and smart to have a flat. I must have read about it somewhere and thought it felt daring.

Another ambition I had – I used to dream about it in my sleeping dreams – was to have a big house and all the rooms different with different periods and nationalities and I had it filled with women, with girls from these countries. A bit like a harem, I suppose. I always loved that dream. The ones that didn't live in, I had enough money to send them tickets to come when they wanted. I was like Lady Bountiful – "Let all the women come!"

They didn't have sex education in school. Perhaps if you were at the grammar school you cut up a rabbit but we cut up flowers. They told us about the stamens and the something-elses of a bluebell. I remember the first time I had a period and my mam sat me on the bed and explained all about it. I think we'd mumbled about it in the school: "You'll have a lot of blood and it's awful." You dreaded this horrible thing you were going to have but I wasn't interested really. It was never coming to me. I don't know how I thought I was going to miss it. It was a shock when it came. I remember being quite frightened and crying and thinking I was bleeding to death.

My mam explained it quite fully then. It was a miracle she said, so I was not to be afraid of it. "Anything else you want to know nearer the time, I'll tell you if you get a boyfriend. This is a monthly thing and it's nothing." I said, "Oh, men get away with it." She said, "But they've to shave every day, haven't they? That's worse. Think of having to shave every day."

"Mam, I'd rather shave than have this thing."

Disposable sanitary towels hadn't been invented then. The old white towels were saved and cut into strips. My mother told me how to fold it and gave me a wide piece of elastic to put round my waist and a couple of safety pins and that was it, get on with it. When you'd finished with it, there was a bucket of salt water with a wooden lid hidden in some place, either in the outside lavatory or under the sink where men never went and you'd put it in there. When there were quite a few, they used to have to be rinsed and rinsed and rinsed and then they would be put in the boiler or in a zinc bucket and boiled with some soap, pegged out on the line. Awful business.

I was allowed as a special treat to stay with my cousin some Saturday nights and I had to sleep in her bed with her. Now, she was very up about sexual matters and she was after telling me this and telling me that: "That's what boys do and it's nice so if a boy takes you out that's what he wants." She was a year younger than me but she knew it all.

As I began to mature and become more independent my dad enforced his discipline even more strictly. The thing that offended him the most was coming in late. I used to be running home saying, "Please God, don't let me dad hit me, please God, don't let me dad hit me." All the way home. But I got hit all the same. If he said, "Come home from the Girl Guides at half past eight," and it was twenty-five to nine, I'd open the door and there he'd be. Silence.

"What time do you call this, madam? What time does it say with that clock?"

He was terrible. I'd say, "Well, we all went round to the chip shop."

"Did you ask your mother if you could go round to the chip shop?"

"No."

"Right." Whack, whack, across my legs.

If he did show a bit of anger, my mother would always plead, "Joe, Joe, that's enough, stop, don't," – like whimpering. He'd say sometimes, "Leave that to me" and sometimes he'd pack it in.

I used to have outbursts. I couldn't stand in front of my dad and defy him so I'd run upstairs shouting, "I'm going to leave home." I had to get upstairs out of his way before I could shout. One night I ran upstairs. My sister, Midge, was in bed. I said, "I'm going to throw myself through this window! I'm not going to stand for this house anymore!" She really thought I was going to do it and she jumped out of bed and held me round the waist.

"Don't, don't throw yourself out the window, Barbara!"

Poor little kid. No wonder she went a bit cranky.

He was just anxious about me, so he told me years later. I was the first-born, remember. I was very important. My cousin got pregnant when she was fifteen which was a terrible disgrace. After that I was hardly allowed out of his sight, he was so afraid of me getting into the same boat.

But when he fell asleep in the evenings, my mother or Midge often used to put the clock back a quarter of an hour. I'd come puffing in, quarter of an hour late. Look at the clock. Look at Midge. Look at my mam. One of them had done it. He never knew.

I gave my mother a fright on one occasion. I'd been reading in a magazine that you could send off for some birth control things – pessaries. The advert made them sound so mysterious and interesting that I thought I'd better write and find what they were about. Not that I'd ever had a fella near me. They came under a plain envelope and I took it up to my room. My mam sees all this literature and says, "What are you sending for those for? Have you been...? Are you er...?"

"No mam, you know me, I'm different from that."

And she dismissed it as curiosity and told me what they were for and how you used them and she hoped I never would have cause to.

4

I Looked at Her Photograph and Fell in Love

I'd just turned fourteen when school broke up for Christmas.
I had Christmas holidays and I went straight to a job in the new
year. When you left school you either went away to be a nurse or
you trained to be a teacher or you had menial jobs to do until you
got married. We had the cotton mills, the tripe factory, the biscuit
factory, office work. My friend Florrie went into a dry-cleaning and
shoe repair shop. Maggie Smith went into a grocer's.

I got an opening in the city dairy. It had started as a little tiny
thing by taking over a dilapidated horse and cart business. In those
days you were still coming out with your jug to get a pint off the
milk cart, dipping into the can with the long-handled measure.
Then you went home and put a little piece of net with beads round
it over the jug to stop the flies getting in.

But we were pushing the bottled milk. It was very advanced.
There was no bottled milk in the whole of Lancashire. We supplied
fancy ice creams as well, and cubes of frozen champagne which
were served at big dinners between courses – so people didn't feel
so bloated and they could eat more. As the business grew, my status
grew. I was in the shop and the office to start with and then they
had someone else in the shop and I was in the office full time.
Sometimes I would go in the very early morning around the farms
collecting the milk, taking little samples which were tested for
butterfat.

I was going to evening classes, night school, to do shorthand, typ-
ing, book-keeping, so that was helping me with my work. That was
one condition on which I was allowed to leave school at the age of

fourteen – evening school four nights out of the five. It didn't matter what the subject was, I must go. My dad wasn't having his daughter lolling about at home or wandering about and getting into mischief.

I loved it. I learnt a lot of different things like drama and art. We'd done drama at school but not to the degree where you dressed up and stood on the stage and recited Romeo and Juliet. I was Romeo. I was just that bit taller so I always took the man's part.

I had a crush on the art teacher. I used to take work out to show her and ask her if this was right or that was right just so as I could lean over and smell her perfume. She was beautiful. I followed her home one night and found where she lived – in a big posh house at the top of Preston Road. I used to go and stand across the street and wonder what window she was at so that I could get a glimpse of her.

My Uncle Jack was a secretary for the Christian Endeavour Friendship Movement and one of his jobs was to welcome any visitors from abroad and to place them with families. So we used to have all kinds of Europeans come through our house and they'd stay a night or two. On one occasion two German boys came, very good-looking, very nice fellas. And one of them showed photographs of his family, showed a photograph of his sister.

As soon as I saw her it was like a fairy story. I just looked at the photograph and fell in love. I thought, God, isn't she one! Oh, isn't she beautiful? He told me her name was Trudi. Before they left, I had got myself an invitation to their home. In due course I went off to Germany. Ten days I think it was. It was a struggle to find the fare for me to go but my father thought if you went abroad it was the best education you could have. Little did he know!

When I saw Trudi in the flesh she was everything – more – than this photo was. And I just fell completely in love with her. But I didn't know quite how to express it. I was quite a kid really. I kept telling her I loved her and how beautiful she was and putting my arms round her and holding her hand walking across the cornfields. That was about all. It was all just very romantic.

After I got home again, a woman started coming into the dairy, very attractive butchy woman. She was twenty perhaps, she seemed ancient to me. I thought she was smashing. She used to come in from a sports club on the outskirts of the town when they were having do's. She'd come and buy a quart of cream. We got chatting.

Then one day she said, "What time do you finish? Which way do you live?" I told her and she said, "I go that way home, would you like a lift?" To have a ride in a car was always a great thrill so she came and picked me up at going home time. She did this a few times. I used to feel all dithery and tingly. We had some lovely country runs just on the outskirts of town. It was wintertime when she said, "Have you been out to a restaurant? Would you like me to take you out somewhere?" Well, at fourteen I hadn't been out to a restaurant so that was another thrill.

And then one evening she said, "Shall we go out a bit further? We'll go for a bit of a run, up to the Yellow Hills." The hills were yellow with gorse in the summer and courting couples used to go up with cars or walking. On the Yellow Hills she stopped the car and started talking.

She said, "You know, you're, you're... a lesbian." She said, "I've watched you." She knew all right. Perhaps the way I spoke, perhaps my manner, although I wasn't one of those butchy kind that stomp about. She said, "You tell me you're more attracted to the women than the men. You're very young – you might grow out of it. But I don't think so. I think you're a born lesbian."

She started to tell me all about lesbians and what lesbians did. I thought, well, this is a lark. My eyes were getting bigger and bigger. I thought, well yes, I do feel like that. There were a few confidences passed. Then she showed me a few things and explained a few things. I had a skirt on – I never wore trousers in those days – and she started fondling with her fingers and saying, "Does this feel nice?" and "Do you like it?" and "Would you like me to go on? There's something else to follow." Then she says, "I'll show you how to do it. You do it to me." So I did it to her and I could hear she's very excited about this and telling me, "Go there," and "a bit further there," and guiding my hand.

So she initiated me. Lovely woman she was, very nice, very kind, nothing vulgar or nasty about her. I was just thrilled to be learning all this. About twice more we went out and she was telling me and teaching me — about women's anatomy really. I wasn't in love with her and she would never've done anything if I hadn't have wanted, although I used to be a bit scared sometimes because I'd never heard of women doing anything like this. And then she must have got frightened because she didn't ask me anymore. Maybe she'd left, gone somewhere else. So that was the end of that little escapade. It's strange how she just seemed to arrive at the right time.

After she'd disappeared I looked all through lots of dictionaries. Could I find lesbian? Finally I found it and it said, 'Of Lesbos.' I thought, God what's this? What's Lesbos? What is it? So I made a few enquiries. "It's a Greek island." Ooh, this must be wonderful if everyone who lives on this island are women! How naive I was. It said something about Sappho so then I had to go to the library

> the hydra which did incalculable evil to Argos.
>
> Spain was a Lerna of ills to all Europe while it aspired to universal monarchy.—*P. Motteux: Preface to Rabelais.*
>
> **Les'bian.** Pertaining to Lesbos, one of the islands of the Greek Archipelago, or to Sappho, the famous poetess of Lesbos, and to the practices attributed to her.
>
> *The Lesbian Poets.* Terpan'der, Alcæ'us, Ari'on, and Sappho, all of Lesbos.
>
> *The Lesbian rule.* A flexible rule used by ancient Greek masons for

Brewer's Dictionary of Phrase and Fable,
second edition.

•

and get a book of Sappho's poems which said she was 'loved by men and women'. I thought, I can't do with all this. I'll just go on my own tack.

But after that my antennae were out more than ever looking at girls' ankles and girls' breasts – and their hair and the nape of their neck I used to love. I'd walk behind them and think what beautiful legs they'd got. I still walk behind women and look.

And now I was sure that when I finally got my flat in London I'd find the streets paved with lesbians, not gold. Well, it was the capital so they must all go there, mustn't they? Going to London sounded like going to America today. You couldn't improve yourself beyond going to London. You wouldn't dream of going to Birmingham or Manchester, you went to the capital. Going to London was a Mecca for me. I love chimney tops and roofs. I wanted life. Never mind getting married and babies. I wanted:

> 1) to have a woman partner
> 2) to have a flat in London
> 3) to have a career.

As our firm grew, we took in more staff and this fella Cyril came as an accountant. He was a queer, what they call a gay now. What's wrong with the word queer? They were called queer in those days. You'd say it: "Oh, do you think he's queer?" or "Do you think she's queer?" Nobody knew what you were talking about really. So along came this queer boy and he was older than me, five or six years and he was a poppet, an absolute treasure. He looked like Robert Donat – one of the film stars, an idol. And he knew it, used to pose sideways so you'd see his profile, and dance like Donat.

He had a boyfriend called Noel that he lived with up Preston Road. They'd got a lovely flat near the park and when you saw Noel in their flat, he was a very different person to what you saw outside. He'd ponce about and he had his apron on and was really such a queen. But another character when he went out round the town.

They were always having fights, always scrapping and then kissing and making up. I remember they had some trouble with another couple because one of them was going to tell Noel's boss that he was a homosexual. The boys used to be awful at gossiping, and jealous of each other. They'd tell tales if they could, one to the other. If they were crossed in love they were like a woman crossed in love, they'd go to any lengths to keep their lover.

My mother liked Cyril because he was a gentle, artistic man, nothing coarse about him. In fact my mother liked him so much, she'd make him a good dinner for sixpence and I'd take it to him in a basin so that he could have it in the office. He was accepted in our home. My parents knew he was different. They knew he'd got a friend but I don't know if they clocked anything, honestly.

If two women lived together down the street, everybody just thought they were two old maids. Nobody knew. I thought afterwards, I bet those two down the street and I'll bet so-and-so... The men had to be rather secretive about it. You didn't get a lot of men living together. It would have looked odd. They'd perhaps be friends and visit each other's homes. For two boys to set up a home, that was quite a nice, brave thing to do. It was never odd for two women to live together.

Cyril was very, very good to me and he knew what was going on very well. I remember him teaching me how to kiss in the dinner hour. He taught me how to kiss properly. I learnt that there's kissing and kissing and there's a thing called a French kiss. He said, "Go to the cinema and watch them. When they're kissing, have a look." I don't know what the boss would have said – giggling our heads off. But it was very serious for me.

For a couple of years I'd been writing to Trudi from time to time, asking her to come and stay. My mother said, "She can stay as long as you want as you've found a nice friend." At last Trudi left school and her parents agreed that she could come to England to learn English.

Midge and I normally shared the one bed in our bedroom; in those days you had double beds so you could put three children at the top and three children at the bottom if you had to. When I went to bed in the evening I'd give Midge a push over into the cold part and I'd get into the warm sheets. She was a very devoted little sister. She'd get up and bring me drinks and whatever I wanted. However, it was arranged that Trudi slept in the bed with me and Midge was turfed out to go and sleep on the couch on the other side of the room, which she heartily hated.

Sharing this bed was another thing. I was able to pass on everything I'd learnt in the Yellow Hills — experimented on Trudi — found Trudi quite liked it. But of course we had to be ever so careful because we'd to wait till my sister was asleep and make sure she wasn't pretending. We daren't make any noise. We found that the best way to do this was me lying on my back gazing up into the air and her lying on her belly next to me with my hand underneath her. That seemed to be the least noise-making action. It was all rather exciting and we really did love each other. She adored me, would do anything. So we learned how to love and how to kiss. Really just experimenting. There were no books and nobody to ask. It was all trial and error; what she liked and what I liked.

Cyril was in the run of things with all the queer boys. He was very popular. Saturday evenings, according to how the money spun out, we used to go with them to Blackpool. It was six shillings on the train. We thought it was expensive, just for the evening. We'd go to the Tower Bar next to the Tower where all the queers used to meet — all men, never did see a woman there. Sometimes we'd go to Manchester to the theatre with Cyril and two others they knew. We saw *Showboat* and *Nymph Errant* with Gertrude Lawrence and all the Noël Coward shows.

I used to know those show-songs off by heart. Cyril had all the records. My favourite always was 'I'll See You Again'. And Cole Porter's 'Experiment', that was a super one. It was about making

***Bitter Sweet* at Manchester Opera House, 1931, featuring 'I'll See You Again'.**

•

love really and experimenting all the time. By then Trudi had told me many times she loved me and I used to sing these songs to her.

We went to operas as well just because it was the thing to do if you'd got the money. You went to all the operas that came, you went to all the shows that came. It was very glamorous to me – to be able to go to Manchester for one thing – dressing up and showing ourselves off and the boys looking after us and me teasing them about their latest conquests.

We'd go to them for supper. First time I'd had candlelight supper in somebody's house. Even then they did things beautiful, they knew how to. All the homosexual boys were so wonderful to me – I think because lesbians were so scarce – and with Trudi as well, they used to show us off, thought we were a dashing pair.

Barbara c. 1933.

5

"You Like Girls Club?"

There's nothing like your first romance. You have more serious ones, perhaps more mature ones but that first one when you're experimenting and it's all fresh and new, it's just wonderful.

It was all a fabulous adventure. I was seventeen by then and Trudi was fifteen. She was just a bit shorter then me, very slender, not properly developed of course at that age. Heart-shaped face, beautiful eyes. She used to put Nivea all over her face and her body and I used to think Nivea made you beautiful because she was beautiful. She'd a lovely mouth and a little very faint hair over her lip which was thought to be attractive in those days. Square shoulders, slender hips, legs not too long, nice bottom. She was good to look at. People stared, turned round and stared.

If I led she'd follow me anywhere to do anything. If I told her to, she'd do it. She'd never remonstrate. But she knew what she wanted. She weren't a namby-pamby. If I said, "Would you like to go?" she'd never say, "Oh well, what do you want to do?" She'd always say yes or no.

We decided we'd get engaged so off we went to a jeweller's shop. It had a pawnbroker's side so they often had unclaimed rings and goods. We looked a long time through the window. She chose a swanky ring with a little diamond and it fitted her so we didn't need to have it altered, which we thought was a good omen. We went in a church and knelt down in the front pew and said a little prayer, and I put the ring on her finger. How innocent we were. So then she was going round with this ring on. All the boys were thrilled, egging us on.

I did definitely take the masculine role then and I wanted to get into tailored clothes. My mother was driven mad going all round the town to find a mannish-looking suit. You could buy a suit off the peg but they weren't the sort I had in mind — I wanted a real tailored suit, a lesbian suit. She said, "I think the best thing is to ask your dad." One of his buddies in the St Cecilia choir was a tailor.

"Ah mam, d'you mean it?"

She said, "Yes, get round to your dad, see if he'll take you to see him."

As a favour to my dad the tailor measured me up and made an exquisite suit very cheaply. That was the first really mannish suit I had. Woollen material, air-force blue with a pinstripe. The skirt fitted over the hips, then very slightly flared. It had a beautiful jacket, padded shoulders and the lining was properly basted so that it wouldn't crumple at the front. It was a great kick to have this. Then of course I had to wear a hat, a navy blue pork-pie hat that went with the suit. I wore that suit to death. I knew I looked right classy in it. Nobody else had a suit made to measure. The boys loved it. They would say, "Get a pink shirt, you want a pink shirt with that sort of costume." Pink was fashionable that year for the men in Blackpool. Pink shirts for men was just hilarious.

I felt a million dollars. It really did something for my ego. It made me feel strong and really butch.

My dad said, "You suit tailored clothes, you don't suit those fussy things." He liked his daughters dressing up and looking beautiful, going out smart. He was proud of us. My mother, I don't think she really knew about lesbians. I don't think anybody really knew about lesbians in those days. They were something that you read about in Greek mythology. It was a long time before 'lesbian' ever got into conversation, and then it was whispered. I don't think it was ever used in our house. You were just one that preferred women's company. If you preferred men you were okay and if you were one of these other ones, you were just a bit odd — "Why should she like women all that much?"

I remember my mam coming home once and she'd found me a little gold watch, a proper little pocket watch, and two rolled gold miniature watch chains, like men used to wear. When I put the chain through the buttonhole at the top of my skirt, I could leave a loop and then put the watch in a little pocket my mother had sewn.

I used to love dressing Trudi up. It was difficult to get clothes. Things were still pretty tight then in our house because we were only working-class people and couldn't spend our money ad lib. Used to make do and mend, look for bargains. I was very nifty with a needle and I loved making hats for Trudi, hats with a bag to match. One hat was supreme – mauve felt, like a fez, with silk anemones all over the top. With her blondie hair and beautiful face and wonderful eyes, she looked terrific.

We were an attractive couple, we really had the gear. The neighbours would open their curtains and go, "Tut, tut, tut, they're out again those two. What they up to now? They're a funny pair. Look what she's wearing. How dare she?" They never classed me as a bad girl or as a tart. They had too much respect for the family. I think they were a little bit in awe really. I mean, it was a tailored suit which only the very rich people could afford.

My parents kept Trudi but they said if I wanted more money, I could get another little job and earn it. She couldn't get a job because she was German. It wasn't allowed. Periodically the police used to come and check up on her, that she was still with us and just a student going to school.

I went to the local photographer. In those days, however poor you were, you always took your children to be photographed every couple of years. It was a big excursion to go and pose. I went to this fella and I said, "I do hear that you can pose for money. I don't want to pose in the nude or anything rude like that, but perhaps you can just like pose with some clothes on or something." He laughed at first. I said, "I want to take some holidays and I haven't got the money." Okay, he would put me on his books. Before long, he sent for me, and the very first thing was a Eugene Hair Perm. They didn't have a lot of perms then. It was just coming into fashion. I thought, Oh God, I don't want to have my hair permed but if I want some money I'll have to start somewhere. I got paid two guineas.

So, to add to all my notoriety, all the hairdresser's shops had this photograph of me – HAVE A EUGENE PERM – in the window to entice people in to have it done. "Gor, that's Barbara Bell! What's she been up to now?" I didn't care. I'd got the two guineas. The best one was a side view with beautiful waves and curls hanging down the back of my neck. From that I got two or three jobs – one was posing for hats – but it was rather unreliable so I had to find a job that was regular. And that was Woolworth's – five shillings, Saturdays, one o'clock to nine o'clock. It was dusty and crowded and hot and of course I wasn't seeing Trudi. She would come in and see me, as long as she dared, round the counter, then she'd go. Nine o'clock, went home. We had about an hour together and then it was bedtime. But that was five shillings all put away, on one side.

I got enough money for us to go to Paris before she went home. Oh God, what a thing that was! We did it in style, absolutely. We booked in a hotel with the very proper name of the Bedford which was near the Madeleine, right central and we didn't see any other English people in it. We did most of it on foot. We had a plan of Paris and we would walk and walk. We did everything. We went to every conceivable thing you could go to. All booked through this hotel.

And did I show off! I'd got a black silk suit my mother had got secondhand from somewhere and Trudi was all done up in chiffon and floral things. We really felt we owned the place. Swaggering into the Opéra, I'd show her to her seat, take her to the bar and order the drinks. I took absolute charge with such aplomb. That was what she did to me. She gave me such confidence, such bravado.

Cyril had given me a couple of addresses where, he'd said, "You'll find your sort of company. You must go to this square where they have stalls and find the soup stall. It's famous for its French onion soup. If you stand there, I'm sure somebody will approach you." So we went to this onion soup stall and up came a fella and said, "You like girls? You like girls club? Come, you follow me."

We wove in and out, round about, for about five minutes, trusting him. Gave him a good tip and he shoved us in a doorway. I didn't know but it was a famous club – Le Monocle. For years and years after that it was still famous. Cyril had warned us. He said, "He'll take you to some sort of a club where you'll be welcomed." He'd never been to it but he knew that there were women's clubs as well as men's clubs and he knew I could look after myself.

There was a red curtain that you went round and then you'd another little red curtain that you'd go round again. Through a maze almost to get into this club. It was old-fashioned and theatrical, quite dark and small but high-class, nothing sordid about it. There were red plush settees all round the sides of the room and the walls were covered with photographs of famous people who had been there. There was a small bar, curved at one side, and a big mirror at the back so you could sit on a stool and see what was going on behind you.

I couldn't tell whether they were men or women sitting on these stools. They were really very butchy and very fem. We fitted in with it all. We didn't look outrageous like they were, but I suppose they dressed up for the evening, a lot of them. The person behind the bar – a very masculine-looking Parisian woman in a suit with her hair Brylcreemed back – turned out to be Lulu, the owner of it. I really thought it was a man. She was there with her girlfriend, and they welcomed us. They spoke English pretty well. We soon made friends, and they showed us to a tiny table in another room through a wideish doorway. There were so many tables, with little lamps, so many women, all lesbian, no men at all. Oh God, was I thrilled! It was out of this world. It was paradise. It was everything I had dreamt of.

When we first arrived, they all flocked round. We were quite a curiosity. There were about forty women – two or three German girls and the rest French. Some of the girls were sitting at the bar working as hostesses. If you wanted you could choose a girl and take her upstairs. I know because I went there later on, after the war.

We went home in a taxi because I'd no idea where we were. We went back three times during that holiday. But we didn't learn any antics. We learned a bit of language and how to recognise other lesbians and what the fashions were – bow-ties were in then for women, for the butch one. That was a wonderful initiation into lesbian life and I remember it so clearly. The dance floor was about six foot square so you couldn't really dance, you just held each other and waggled about. To see women kissing when they were dancing, I thought, God! Where am I? I knew I was in Paris but I felt I was on another planet.

After a year in Blackburn, Trudi had to go home. I went back with her and stayed the few days that were left of my holidays. Her mother was a housewife and her father was a workman. I remember how spotless their flat was. My mother said that was because they were German. Just to please Trudi's mother while I was there, I had to wear a femmy dress with puffed sleeves and a low heart-shaped neck and a little white apron tied round my waist. Also she knit me – as a great big treat – a Hitler Youth cardigan which was black with a little red and green border and edelweiss buttons. All the youth were wearing them when I was there. They grew up with Nazi beliefs and ideas. It was like joining the Girl Guides here. You joined the Hitler Youth movement, just the natural thing to do. There was no alternative anyway. If you didn't join it, you were out of it all.

And I remember on one occasion when I was there, we were riding in an open-topped car out in the country and there was a big expanse of huts with barbed wire twirled round the perimeter. It seemed to go on for ever and ever. I asked what it was but I was told they didn't know. There must have been something going on there. One can imagine.

All too soon I had to go home and then of course, Trudi and I were writing and trying to get to each other. I hadn't the money, she hadn't the time but I was still desperately in love with her. I would write her out all the songs I used to sing to her:

> Time may lie heavy between,
> But what has been
> Is past forgetting.

I met her in Cologne once again. We stayed in a hotel and were just romancing the whole time. In bed half the time. But we couldn't keep it up by correspondence. After a few years the letters got less and less frequent. I was eating my heart out for her but it more or less dwindled out. I was all ready for it to go on – "We will live together and we will have a home together" – but it was very unrealistic really. She'd got to stay there with her family.

The Nazis were becoming dominant then and I don't doubt they used her. I remember Trudi writing that she'd had to see one of the officers of her region when she got back, had two hours of questioning of what she'd done and what she'd seen and where she'd been. She was so filled with information and she was so keen to be a good Nazi girl. My sister, Midge, is convinced that she was a spy during the war. She had everything at her fingertips to be a good spy. She could have been. She was very intelligent. She spoke perfect English with a Lancashire accent. She knew every English custom. That's why I always felt during the war that I might see her walking down Regent Street posing as an English girl or dropped by parachute somewhere.

My brother Stanley was killed in the war and my love for Trudi turned to hate. I used to think that if I saw her I'd kill her. I'd strangle her. All the sorrow of the war and the horrors of Nazism were put onto poor Trudi. She'd done it all. She was a German. It was her fault. It took me, oh a long time, to forgive her – years – and Midge still hasn't.

I'm still in touch with her. She married an SS officer and had a child by him. He wanted to take the child and bring it up as a little soldier, and she wouldn't allow it. He used to beat her and chuck them out the flat and leave them on the pavement howling. I believe he was very, very brutal to her and because of that it softened my heart towards her.

But we've decided that we really don't want to meet again because it would just shatter a dream. I want to think of her as the beautiful young maiden that I knew. Her voice is the same, and I can tell when she's laughing on the phone. Her voice laughs. It's still the same husky laughing voice. Some years ago her son came to Brighton. And he said, "My mother's told me everything about you. It was the happiest time in her life. She still loves you and she still wears the ring you bought her."

6

Lonely in Blackburn

After Trudi had gone I was very lonely in Blackburn. I was looking out for another partner. I was looking all the time. I didn't know any other lesbians.

Most of my schoolfriends were courting or getting married, though I did have two friends that didn't. One was Florrie. We used to go for walks like girls did in those days or go to the park and sit on a bench and chat. There was a bond between us but I never felt sexy towards her. The other friend – Jenny – was a nurse. Looking back she was definitely lesbian. She was very butch – although I didn't know the word butch then – and wore Vitapointe in her hair to make it shiny. She hated men and she was looking for a woman to live with. We used to talk about women but we didn't say the word lesbian. It was a silent world. They had no words for things then. Just deeds, not words. It was so hush-hush. I never dreamt that one day we'd all be walking about holding hands freely and standing on corners and kissing in the open air. I could never have forecast the freedom that there is today.

It amazes me that there are now so many publications. You can go in a bookshop and find shelves of women's stories and their love affairs and their lives. You could read about lesbians every day for weeks if you wanted but in those days you never saw a thing. There were no books or articles. Cyril did lend me his copy of *The Well of Loneliness* which had been banned in this country and was very difficult to get hold of. He must have smuggled a copy back from Paris. It was a revelation to me. It was a light in my dark world, a sort of beacon. I thought, I must have a relationship like this. If only I could have a life like this. But it was a bit beyond me because the

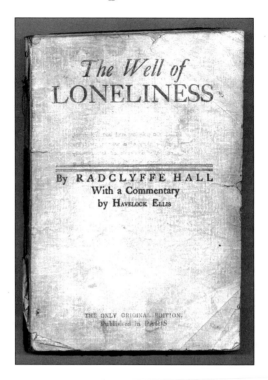

**Cheap, pirate edition of *The Well of Loneliness*,
published in Paris.**

•

characters were rich people who had leisure and could please themselves what they did – nobody pointed a finger. They were just thought to be a bit weird, a bit arty. I thought that kind of life wouldn't come my way.

I was still going out with the boys, the homosexual boys. If you can't find women, you go with the men. If it hadn't been for them I'd have gone up the wall during those years in Blackburn. From that time to now I've always had gay friends, always. They were my allies. The Girl Guides and the gay boys were the only people I could identify with really.

I'd already had a nice little interlude with the Guides a couple of years before. I couldn't have Wakes Week holiday with everyone else when the whole town closed down because the dairy had to go on serving milk. They said, "You can have any other week." I couldn't go on holiday with the family so I advertised in *The Guider*. Would some Guide company going camping adopt a Girl Guide from Blackburn for a week? And I went with a troop of strangers from Selly Oak in Birmingham.

It was raining very hard one night and the Guider said, "Run as fast as you can. Take all your bedding and run into the hut and get down to sleep. Put your bedding anywhere. Get close together, cuddle up." I thought, rather – suits me! And two of us were a bit cold so I said, "Come on, get into me sleeping bag, you'll soon get warm." We had a nice little feel around and the next day we were holding hands and going behind the bushes. Having a little kiss or a little feel. Lovely. When I was seventeen I joined the Rangers which I enjoyed very much because there were always a lot of latent lesbians in the Rangers.

It was the fashion then – every church had a brownie pack so the vicar appealed for someone to start a pack at our church. My mam and dad were always encouraging me to help others so I became a Brown Owl. I did that for six years and I loved it. I'd got all the little ones to shove around which I adored. We had four sixes – Pixies, Gnomes, Fairies and Elves. And my mother, I don't know where she found a stuffed owl in a glass case but it came out of the case and she cleaned it all up. This owl used to sit on a toadstool – which we had bought from the Guide movement – while we went round it singing, "Twit, twit twoo, twit, twit twoo". And then the meeting was open.

There was great competition in the sixes. You taught them about baby matters and flower growing, how to wash their knickers and their vest. How to Make a Bed. How to Clean Your Teeth – and how often. How to Roll Your Clothes Up – so they didn't get

Camping holiday, Maggie Smith far left.

•

creased. How to Do Up a Parcel. How to Dial 999 in an Emergency.

The Brownie Commissioners were usually titled ladies. They were really out of my world. They set an example of courtesy and politeness. They would always remember to bring something if you were having a jumble sale. One of them used to bring beautiful shoes she'd bought at Kendall Mills in Manchester – a very swanky shop. I was the first one to have these shoes. They were excellent quality.

I liked that particular Commissioner – she didn't talk down to the children and she came to visit us even in camp. We used to go to camp every year. One year we went to a holiday camp at Lytham St Anne's, near Blackpool. That was a special excitement because we'd never seen a holiday camp before. Rows and rows of chalets all joined together. They all had balconies and little fences. Some of the children had never seen the sea before, either.

Another time we camped out in a farmer's field. The farmer had two daughters that I used to go dancing with. I should think the elder one might have been a lesbian – great thumping creature and a bit rough, never had any time for men. She knew a lot about botany and she'd explain to the children what the flowers were called and why they grew where they did. If you were stung by one there was another next to it that counteracted the sting. They learnt a lot. I learnt a lot too.

To pass the long evenings I'd often go to the cinema with my friend Florrie. If you went to the top bedroom in our house with a pair of binoculars you could see what was on at the Roxy which was the local fleapit. Greta Garbo and Marlene Dietrich were my favourites. When *Dracula* came out there was a prize offered to anyone who could sit through the film all on their own without screaming and running out. It was supposed to be very frightening. I put my name down and I was picked out to go down to the cinema at quarter to eleven at night. There was a big crowd of people waiting outside to see me go in. In I went with a bag of sweets and a bag of peanuts and sat in the middle of the cinema on my own and watched the film. If it was a bit horrible, I just shut my eyes. When I came out there were a few stragglers left on the pavement. They gave a clap and a bit of a cheer and my dad was waiting to take me home. I won a token for a perm, which I gave to my mam.

Dancing was another distraction and I threw myself into it with real vigour. I loved dancing, was a good dancer. Cyril used to do my hair for me, comb it, cut it. I did have beautiful hair, golden red and he'd turn it round the bottom so it was a perfect long bob or sometimes he'd set it at the front with his fingers. Occasionally he'd come to do my mother's hair with his curling tongs. And he was well into make-up. He taught me how to use make-up for dances.

They don't have balls now – this jigging around and standing drinking from the bottle, I think it's disgusting. Thursday night in winter was the ball night. Grocers' ball. Policemen's ball. Farmers' ball. The girls used to stand up like wallflowers near the bar, waiting for a man to come up and ask them to dance – ridiculous. You could dance with the women. They didn't frown on it. Half the evening I'd be dancing with one or two girls that were good dancers or good-looking. You got the thrill of dancing with a woman, actually being close to one – but that was about as far as it went.

You'd always get the odd fella, some traveller to the town, who'd come to the ball and thought he'd get a cheap pick-up. There was one dance, a slow foxtrot, where you could get a bit close and cuddle a bit or smooch and you'd feel him getting hard and patting your bottom and thinking he was going to take you out the back door and have a quick one. You'd think, oh God, another of them! You'd say, "Sorry, I don't want to dance with you, excuse me," and leave him there. I just used to laugh at them.

I had fellas chasing after me, asking if they could take me home. You knew what they were after and you thought, well I'll have to play this clever. Because you knew invariably they would stop round the corner from where you lived and start putting their hand all round your bosom and you'd think, oh hell, same old thing and you'd say, "Sorry, I don't like that."

"Oh you're a funny one."

But I never fell for any of the men. Just used to like them for what I could get out of them, learn from them. I'd be taken for an interesting car-ride in the country or a jolly good meal. If I didn't know what I should be doing my mother would say, "Start with the outside knife and fork and watch what they do and you'll be all right. Mustn't be shy. Doesn't mean to say because they have money you're not as good as they are."

So I had boyfriends. My mother thought it was healthy. But it was all an act to me, just an act. They only had to undo the buttons of my blouse once and they'd had it.

With the dairy we used to go to exhibitions and have a stall with literature about milk and its food values, which people had never heard about. On one of these occasions on the next stand there was a Manchester Jew called Lewie. This guy made a beeline for me. Did I like eating because he knew some beautiful fish restaurants. I dolled up and went. He was a kind man. He taught me a lot. Told me how to fillet a fish on your plate. You didn't go plouff! in a piece of fish and show your ignorance, show your upbringing. You'd want to be a bit above that.

Each time I met him, he gave me a little enamelled dog that was gold underneath, solid gold. I got three of these, very expensive things and I used to wear them round my neck on a little gold chain.

Some of Lewie's friends were in the rag trade and one of them asked me if I had ever considered being a model. Well, *mannequin* shot through my brain. This fella said he saw how I held myself when I was dancing and he would train me if I would go into his fashion house. I said, "I really will have to see what me parents say." We-e-e-ll, all hell broke loose because they thought this Jew man was enticing me into the wicked world. Next time he called for me, my dad said, "You leave this house and you never see me daughter again," and he marched him to the front door. Lewie told me afterwards he'd asked my father for his permission to marry me. He'd tried to convince him that he'd make a good husband. But you'd have thought it was the devil himself asking for permission. It was just because he was a Jew. He could have been a millionaire but if he was a Jew that was it. It was most unkind. I bled my heart out. That was the end of Lewie, the end of the little gold charms.

Somehow Cyril got to know two lesbians that lived outside Preston. He took me to meet them. Summer evening it was, went on the bus. They were Jan and Bert — Jan and Bertha. Jan was much older than Bert and she was a perfect housewife. Bert had brogue shoes that were highly polished and tailored jackets and skirts. She wore nice fitted collars and ties and she had short hair. She used to go out to work to Preston in her father's business every day. They were very, very happy.

We were walking round the garden and I was walking behind with Bert, the butchy one, talking about the flowers. Cyril was walking with the nice femmy one in front and I heard this Jan saying, "Of course she is, you only need to look once at her! Surely you didn't doubt it did you?" I thought, oh good, I'm passed. I felt so bucked, I felt so proud. I thought, at last I'm recognised, I don't have to have horns or a halo, I'm just a woman and I'm a lesbian woman and I'm accepted, they think I'm all right. We went many times after that. I thought, if I could only live like these two, I'd be so happy.

I was still missing Trudi. Cyril said, "Look, she's gone home. She's put her trunk in the wardrobe. She's put you in the trunk. She's forgotten you, love. All you can do is to look for somebody else. That's the cure for a broken heart. You'll find somebody. You'll get over it. Get out of Blackburn, go somewhere else."

I thought he was heartless but I was ready to go, to leave home then. In the evenings I liked to fiddle with the wireless until I got a foreign station and imagine the gabbling was Chinese. I always wanted to go to China. My mother would say, "Maybe you'll go there one day." I used to listen to all this gabble and be thrilled, thinking I was listening to something from the other side of the world. I just wanted to get away from Blackburn, get away from home. I did once think I'd like to go to Australia because you could get an assisted passage to Australia then. And then we had a missionary that was in Africa somewhere and I said, "How can I be a missionary? How can I join you?" He said the best thing was to get a nurse's training. That was too much fag. I wanted to go there and then.

I had already made a few abortive attempts to leave. A big dance band were looking for a singer. It was the rage coming in then to have a singer. Cyril said, "Go for it, send them one of your photographs." I had a little practice singing in the office and I asked the boss if I could change my half-day to go to the audition. I was all secretive. I could hardly tell my parents about this adventure. And then it came out.

"Oh your Barbara's changed shifts."

God, did I get told off for that. My parents were very strict. I think if they hadn't been I might have been a naughty girl. I had it in me because I'd got real spirit. If I thought something was glamorous I easily fell for it. My dad wasn't going to have his daughter singing with a band. I was forbidden to go.

And then the other time was when I answered an advert in *The Lady* for a mother's help, sounded some grand place down South. My mother said, "Do you want to go away from home? I thought you were happy here. I know you've to leave sometime but why didn't you say you wanted to go? We'll find something for you if you want to go away." She said, "Don't tell your Dad" – it was always "Don't tell your Dad – he might be upset."

Nobody could speak when my father came home from work. He was reading the paper. If he wanted to read little bits out to you then that was a bonus. You could have the paper after he'd had it, but he had to open it new. He knew I was restless. He said one night, "Now here's something you could do, Barbara, if you put your mind to it. You could go and be a London policewoman. Look what this policewoman has done" – she'd won an award for bravery or something.

"Do you think I could?"

"Why not," he said, "you'll never know if you don't try." He was always pushing us on to better ourselves.

My parents thought it was a good idea for me to find work somewhere else. I was approaching twenty-three. I was obviously not going to have much of a career in Blackburn. I was obviously not going to marry anybody. The aunts were still asking my mother, "Ee, Beattie, when's your Barbara going to wed then? She'll finish up an old maid, you know." My mother would say, "When she's ready she'll choose somebody so let the matter drop." And then she'd give me a little twinkle, as much as to say, "Don't take any notice of them, love." She had very advanced ideas and she accepted me, always sticking up for me and never a wrong word.

So off I wrote to Scotland Yard. I had a very nice letter saying: "When you are twenty-four years of age apply again." You had to be fit and healthy, have so many of your own teeth, your eyesight at so many yards and sit an entrance examination.

"How am I going to do this, Dad?" I said.

"Well," he said, "you've got a year. I'll speak to Miss Dent at choir tonight."

Miss Dent, my favourite teacher, came to the rescue. When I finished work I used to go home for my dinner and then I'd go up to Miss Dent's for English, arithmetic and general knowledge. Of course, that was bliss. She never said anything to me, but I always felt that she liked me and I'd always adored her. She sent for past exam papers and coached me to an excellent standard. So when it came to my twenty-fourth birthday the application forms came from the Met. They were all filled in with the help of Miss Dent and off they went. The local police came to spy on the home background, the family and everything, because they were very particular in those days.

Very soon I was called up for an interview. I think out of more than twenty women sitting there in Scotland Yard they chose three of us. The next day we had to go over to Burlington House to sit the exam and, of course, I passed it, which I knew I would. I just had to wait to be called to enter the training college which was near Westminster Hospital – Peel House.

It was still very unusual for a woman to become a police officer. They certainly didn't have them in Blackburn. Everybody made a great fuss and the minister of our church held a special service to bless me. He gave a little lecture and we said a few prayers, sang a hymn. Everyone shook my hand and gave me a kiss. There was many an occasion when this blessing flashed back to me, on the beat in London. They made me feel that I was being protected, not just by their prayers but by some power.

I was in the local newspaper, front page. There was a photograph. My father kept budgies, so it was me with a budgie sitting on my shoulder. It said, 'It's a fair cop' and that I was going to the Great Metropolis. My dad was very proud and quite boastful, couldn't have been a prouder man in Blackburn. My mother was always more placid about these things. My aunts and the neighbours were aghast – "Eh, I wouldn't let any lass of mine go down to London." Going to London was considered very daring and an insult to Lancashire. What was wrong with staying in Blackburn? They thought London was a wicked place. But they didn't know how wicked!

I thought I'd find everything in London and I'd try to achieve my three ambitions – a flat, a profession and a girlfriend. I was sure I would find somebody in London and I instinctively knew that I would find somebody in the police.

7

On the Beat

There were two other women in the police school when I was there. One of them was a great big solid woman and always reliable if you went out on the beat. The other one was matter-of-fact. We did everything the men did: square-bashing and marching. Every fortnight we had an exam and we three women were always the top three. I loved it. It was freedom, although it was restricted freedom because I had to live in what was called a section house over Wandsworth. Eventually we were all sworn in to serve King and Country. Then you were posted to a station.

When you got into uniform it did make you feel different. You did feel you had power and authority and you felt you had respect – which you had in those days. The policeman was a friend. You helped people. Everybody would say good morning or good afternoon. People would stop you on the beat because they wanted to have their photograph taken standing next to a policewoman.

The uniforms were rather quaint. The skirts were well mid-calf, so they came over your boots. And the boots were beautiful – thin fitted calf, custom-made. A fella used to come from Northampton to measure you for them. It was spit and polish to get them shining. We had to be turned out smart. No slappy-dashy, no hair flopping around like they have today. Your hair had to be up or tied back and tucked under your hat. In the beginning they were like a kind of pith helmet and then in the war when the air-raids started we got the tin hat. After the war we got caps with a peak – very smart.

My first posting was to Vine Street, a little tiny street between Piccadilly and Regent Street, next to Veeraswamy's Indian

Restaurant where the Indian doorman would stand, dressed up in all his regalia. You'd pass him and exchange a word then go up some grimy stairs in a little passage to the station.

When you first joined you didn't go out on your own for weeks, you went out with another officer to show you the ropes. My escort was a Scot from a millionaire's family. She had joined the force at the same time as her girlfriend, who was the daughter of her father's gardener. They wanted to be together. There was a great hoo-ha about it in the *News of the World*. She was a topping woman. We did a lot of work together later on in plain clothes.

Policewomen's duties included any work to do with women or children. Often women would talk to a policewoman or do things for a policewoman when they wouldn't for a man. We were on station duty, looking after women in the cells. We were escorting girls to approved schools, looking for missing girls and later, girls in the forces who were absent without leave. We'd be called to domestic incidents, rowing about the children or one of them always drunk and no money. If there was a woman involved we had to go.

I used to love it on the beat. I felt I was doing a good job and I was very happy doing it. You hadn't to appear to be scared but inside sometimes there was a little fear of the unknown. Rows outside pubs were quite frequent. You were told at the college that if you were out on the beat and somebody came running and said, "Hey, there's a fight," you'd to walk as slow as you could because when you got there you bet your life they'd fought it out and agreed. If you went and pushed yourself in the middle of a fight you got the worst of it. You never went rushing to a fight.

I was fortunate in going to different areas – Limehouse, Paddington, Southwark, Savile Row, Marlborough Street, Bow Street. It was quite different being stationed at Leman Street off Aldgate from being in the West End. There was lots of drug trafficking round the dock area in Limehouse. The police would often raid Chinese lodging houses and they would always take a police-woman with them in case there were women there to be searched. I was given a taste of cannabis and a little lesson about cocaine and opium because I'd never come across them myself.

When I was at West End Central we had the prostitutes. The high-class ones used to stand along Piccadilly and the streets in Shepherd's Market and oh, were they smart! Were they beautiful! I never knew a nasty one. Some of them would have a little pet poodle trotting along beside them. Then you got the cheaper ones around Lisle Street on the other side of Piccadilly Circus. You used to get a few nasty ones there. They had to fight a bit harder. They were often poor little scrappy things that had some man controlling them.

The prostitutes would always help you during the war if you had a bit of a struggle, or if you wanted a message taken – you could always rely on them. You'd go in a deep doorway when the bombs were falling and have a good chitty-chat, tell stories. Often they were on the game to support a child because they wanted them to be brought up properly or go to some good school. There was a shelter at the bottom of Bond Street and, of course, all the Bond Street girls used to come trotting down there, ping, ping, ping. I've seen them more than once take off a fur coat and wrap it round a woman with her baby and say, "No, you keep it, I was tired of that mink."

Sometimes you'd stand in the doorways with them and they'd say, "Oh well, I'd better get on my beat now," and go trotting off. I'd call out after them, "You keep out of my way because if I see you making a nuisance of yourself you're in." And they would say, "Well, I haven't been in for a long time have I?"

"No, but you're pretty well due so you watch out."

If they got a bit bolshy then you'd have to take them in. But what did they get? Fined two pounds, which was nothing to them. Just a bore to have to get up in the morning to come to court.

Piccadilly Circus after a bombing raid.

There was one prostitute had bleached white hair. She was as thin as a skeleton and we called her The Ghost. She just used to wear a little tiny pair of panties underneath her fur coat and she'd stand there in the doorway and open her coat, shut it. Sometimes she would have the maid coming running and then they'd both go back quickly to the flat because a punter had called. There was another one called Maurie, a big woman, beautiful – she was a lesbian. She used to do it because she wanted to give her partner everything, because she loved her.

I'd never seen a prostitute before. A lot of things were strange to me, coming from the provinces. It was a bit like never having seen a lesbian before. I thought she might have horns or something different, but she just looked like any other woman. Perhaps I should have been a prostitute. I always felt something in common with them.

I went in one place with the men and found a sort of torture chamber. There were rings on the floor and chains on the wall. That was an eye opener for me. When the girls were talking to me in the doorway they used to tell me what funny things the men would want. There was one used to bring a load of Lyons cream buns. She had to walk round the room and he used to chuck these cream buns at her. He didn't want sex. The buns used to give him a kick. And they'd tell me about funny things they'd to do in the bath.

We had a lot of girls run away from home and hanging around the West End. You had a sort of sixth sense if you saw somebody in a club or hanging about with the prostitutes or sitting in the cafés very early in the morning or in the lavatories having a wash. You had a way of coaxing them into a phone box and you'd dial CRO for the Criminal Record Office, say the name she'd given you – which was often wrong – and a date of birth and any other peculiarities and they would tell you if she was missing.

Sometimes they might be wanted for some offence in another town and we would have to take them there by train. You got the guard to lock the doors of your compartment and then when you were at your station he'd come and unlock them. If the girls were underage we sometimes had to take them before the court as being in need of care and protection or beyond parental control and then the poor things would be sent to an approved school. If they were over sixteen and they didn't want to go home you'd say, "Can we write to your mother and tell her that we know you're all right?" Sometimes they'd be thankful and say, "Oh yes, oh I'm glad it's all come out, will you get them to come for me?" All was forgiven all round. We got a lot of rewards, as well as seeing a lot of nasty things.

They often went on the streets. You knew that and they knew you knew that. You used to shut your eyes to a lot of it. There used to be little fights if somebody new came on to a prostitute's patch but the older ones were very motherly to them and gave them a start. Then you got horrible ponces that sent them out and took the money off them. Occasionally you would get young girls shut up in some man's room. They loved getting the young girls and they would lock them up and never let them out. A neighbour might tell you that they thought there was a young girl in there or they'd seen her going out and she looked so scared all the time. But often they didn't want to leave because they were so well looked after.

There were quite a few lesbians in the police circle. We weren't all lesbians. You still got the ones that were all sexy eyes for the fellas. But you didn't have little namby-pamby girls joining the police force. They had to have a certain force of character to want to join in the first place. And to be accepted they had to have something forceful and decisive about them. A lot of the lesbians, like me, had joined the force because they were wanting to find a partner or have some flutter. There was a lot of creeping into each other's rooms at the section house.

I'd made great friends with a woman called Tonks. She was brought in as a rookie and I had to carry her round the beat. She was always calm. I felt if there was any crisis she'd know what to do. She had that confident manner and she became a very good policewoman. I was always rather a fan of hers. She was responsible, with a friend of hers, for tracking down the Acid Bath murderer after the war. There were another two I used to visit quite frequently. One of them had worked for Molyneux as a dressmaker. She used to make her lover's suits, beautiful tailored costumes, so her friend always looked a little bit superior. I thought, ooh, at last I've found two women living together in London!

We used to meet up after work, sometimes a little gang of us which was super. There was a place we used to go to for amusement, called Gunter's, off Park Lane. It's gone now. A lot of women used to go there. It was expensive, and posh, rather colonial style. Real tearooms but you could always pick up – if you wanted – some bored rich woman dripping with gold and jewels. I never did, but I had plenty of opportunity. The little waitress would come over and say, "The lady over there – would you like to join her for tea at her table?"

"Yes, certainly" – crikey.

But I'd just have tea and thank them and then buzz off.

By joining the police I'd achieved one of my ambitions. I'd got a profession. So now I had to look for a partner. At a promenade concert one night, I met an interesting woman. We were sitting up in the gallery, a little group of us from the police and I was introduced to her. She was Vic Adams, a New Zealander and we struck up a friendship. She was very clean and intelligent, and very masculine. She looked like a boy, like a young boy. She had her hair cropped and wore men's clothes: trousers, underpants, socks and the lot and always the same kind of brogue shoes. She used to ring up Harrods and say in a deep voice, "Could I have another pair of size six brogues, please?" She cultivated this deep voice. She really was posing as a man. She used to strap her bosom down with calico, pieces of material with tapes on. She'd strap it down, then pull these tapes round the front. It seemed to be quite professionally made. It was rather strange. She just didn't like the idea that she had breasts, I suppose. I never mentioned it. I was tactful enough not to because it might have been a sore point with her. I found her a bit of a novelty because she was so butch. I'd never met a creature like her. She wasn't much of an advert for lesbianism but she took a fancy to me.

She was desperate for a girlfriend but she couldn't openly seek a partner in New Zealand. It was so frowned upon. She had a farm with her brother over there but she said the people would not accept her so she had left the farm and was travelling the world looking for a girlfriend. She wanted to build a house for me in New Zealand and we would live quietly there, pretending I was her long-lost English cousin.

The fact that she thought I was the one for her was very attractive but I didn't know if we would get on, so we went off to Ireland for a holiday to see how things went. She asked if she could take a tent and I said, "You'll have to pitch it, I want comfort." So I used to sit in the car while she was putting up the tent. We did go to bed and breakfast places as well but when we asked, "Have you got a bedroom please for two", they'd give us a look because they thought I was with a fella and in those days you didn't sleep two, male and female together like they do now. We had to keep going back to the tent because they kept saying no, they hadn't a room. We did more of the tent than we did the rooms in the end.

She had a powerful car and we would pick out little tracks on the map, go down to the seashore. Often we swam in the bays – swam naked and came out naked and made love naked because there was just not a soul about. She was very good at making love.

But I didn't fancy life in New Zealand. I would have been completely in her hands which I didn't like the thought of. I didn't want to have to ask her for money for a bar of chocolate or a sanitary towel. Most of the women that I've met, they've always wanted to take care of me.

"Oh, you'll be free, you can do what you like but just let me look after you and give you all the things you should have."

But you're no more free than jump in the air. And as for looking after me, I'm very capable. I can look after myself. But I seem to have brought that out in women that I've met. Vic did find a girlfriend in the end – a nanny her brother had got for his children. So there she was, right on her doorstep all the time.

8

As Happy as a Sandboy

I'd fleetingly seen a cherub-looking girl when we'd been training at Peel House. Beautiful blonde hair and milky white complexion, sort of rounded all over. Very feminine-looking girl. I thought, how did you get in the police?! We'd had hardly any time to talk.

Then one night when I was working in my cubicle at the section house I heard muffled crying. I thought, it's that woman next to me, that cherub. I wonder what's upset her. We can't have this. I'll have to see what's up. So I stood on my bed and peeped over the top and I said, "I'm in the next cubicle, what's the matter?" She said, "I'm homesick." I said, "Poor kid. Do you want me to come round and talk to you?" She said, "Yes, please."

Well, I had to get out of this one door and into another door without anybody knowing or the door creaking. It was terrible in the section house. It was like being in a boarding school. The sergeant used to stand at the door and say, "Lights out, girls. No more talking." I said, "Well, where have you come from, anyway?" She'd come from Lancashire and her name was Madeleine. She stopped crying and we had a little bit of a talk. I said, "Would you like me to get into bed with you?" She said, "Oh, yes please." We only had tiny single beds and you had to lie close else you'd fall out. We had the night together and I consoled her in more ways than one.

I was still looking for somebody that I could live with for the rest of my life, somebody I could really fall in love with. I thought, perhaps this is the one I've come to meet.

Soon after that Madeleine was posted to a beautiful section house in Pembridge Square off Notting Hill Gate. She heard that I was

16 and 17, Pembridge Square today.

•

being posted too. She immediately went to the sergeant in charge and said, "I know her, she comes from my part of the country – can we share a room together?" So when I got there it was a *fait accompli*...

Anyway it was a beautiful room at the back of the house. In the distance you could see Notting Hill, the high street. We had a balcony we could climb out on to and we eventually had it filled with flowers. From then on the relationship just bloomed. I fell completely and utterly in love. I thought, it's Fate. She must be the one. She was so pretty. She was feminine but she was very practical, which I liked. She used to like dressing up, not so much as I did but she looked good in clothes. And good out of clothes. We decided at the first opportunity to get a flat together.

You were supposed to live in the section house for a year – it was the custom – to prove that you were a worthy person before you were allowed to live out. But the war came and they were anxious to move us out to let in new recruits. Women could enlist for any of the forces, including the police force. They hoped they were going to have a big intake of women into the police so Madeleine and I were given the option to move out of the section house if we wished.

We were all waiting for bombs to come. We were all waiting for the big noise. We thought they were going to start any minute but we didn't have bombs for nearly a year.

We went to William Whiteleys and got a flat in Westbourne Grove, over the Britannic Assurance Company. We'd nothing when we moved into it except a few things we'd bought with our monthly pay. We'd got the necessities like brooms and brushes that you must start off with, a few knives and forks. We had a chicken-yellow carpet which we bought from somewhere and a cushion or two. It was difficult to get furniture. We got some boxes about fourteen inches square that had held butter because butter was sold loose then. I put hinges on, made a handle. Madeleine covered them with chintz, little padded top. So we had two stools. We used to lift the top and put things inside them. We bought a dressing table and pulled the drawers out, turned them up and stood them at the back one on top of the other, painted it up and we had a beautiful little kitchen dresser. We had a bath in the kitchen that had a wooden top which came down so that you could use the top as a workbase. Whenever you wanted a bath you'd to clear everything off and lift up this enormous lid and fasten it with two little bolts against the wall.

My parents were thrilled that I was getting a flat of my own with a lovely woman from the police force. We went on a begging tour. Uncle Jack gave me something and my dad was asking all the relatives. They were all giving things for Barbara's flat. Madeleine's mother gave us a beautiful bedroom suite and helped with the curtains. My dad arranged for a little van to pick them all up. In the meantime I'd seen two chairs in a junk shop in Preston. They had black brocade with flowers on. They were very, very old and all torn.

You could see the horsehair inside. They had five shillings written on in chalk – I'd gone to buy a bicycle, mind you – I said to the shopkeeper, "Only five shillings?" He said, "Some bugger's rubbed off the two. They're twenty-five shillings for the pair. They're loving chairs. You can sit in them and put your arms round your sweetheart." Well, that clinched it. I said, "I'll have them." So my dad called and collected them and all this lot came up like a house removal.

We got a great big double bed, which was heaven and a big double wardrobe in the bedroom. We made a beautiful home. I'd got my flat in London at last. I'd got my career. I'd got my girlfriend and we loved each other very dearly. I'd got the lot. I'd achieved my three ambitions. By then I was twenty-five. It had been a long time to wait but it was worth it. I was as happy as a sandboy.

In the course of my duties in Mayfair, I accidentally found a lesbian club. I kept quiet, kept it to myself. I'd go there with Madeleine if we wanted a night out. It was a very high-class club in Hertford Street – beautiful club, beautiful clients, all women. It was secluded and secretive, very posho, rather like Le Monocle. Red plush and comfortable and luxurious. There was also the Gateway which was low-class compared with this one, all right in its way but I only went there two or three times. Sometimes I used to go in the men's pubs just to be with some queers, that was all. Didn't know any pubs where women went.

The police raided the Mayfair club one night when we were in and took our names. I gave my club name which was the name of the street in which I was born so that if I was a bit blotto it always came to my rescue – Barbara Johnston. They didn't take anybody away. They just had a good poke around to see if there was anything going on that shouldn't be – non-members who hadn't been signed in by a member. So off they went with all the record books and we thought that was the end of it.

A week or two later our superintendent wanted to see us. Now that was the highest rank of the women police, was the woman superintendent. She was a fine woman, principled – very butchy but nice with it. I don't know why people think that if they're a butch lesbian they have to go around spitting. They can be quite gentle people underneath. We were called to see Superintendent Peto.

"God, what does she want us for?"

You didn't go and see her unless it was something very, very serious. It came out we'd been found in this place. So she gave us a little lecture and then she said, "You're a silly pair of young puppies. Why didn't you tell me you wanted a club, you could have come to my club." We cleared out with our tails between our legs and "Sorry ma'am". We never did find out which was her club.

What a woman she was! She was proud of us all. We were her 'gels'. She knew who were lesbians and who weren't. I don't think she really minded so long as you did your job well. She liked to choose her girls. She hand-picked the ones that she thought would be sensible and wouldn't marry and leave the force after the country had spent so much money in training them. Every few months you were transferred to another station so that there was no fear of you being swept up by some fella which was great for me because I met new women. Didn't matter being swept up by some woman.

At Vine Street there were a couple of other butchy lesbians and at break time we used to sit outside on the fire escape, puffing at our pipes. We thought it was a bit daring to have pipes and it was cheaper and easier to get loose tobacco than cigarettes. They were elegant little briar pipes – I've still got them – a Major Dash and a Dr Plumb. One girl I liked came from Devon, beautiful skin and a deep voice – she was a real butchy girl and she used to smoke Capstan Full Strength cigarettes, so I thought, oh, I'd better go on to Capstan Full Strength as well. They were foul!

There was a sort of uniform for lesbians then. If you were the butchy one you would dress mannish. You wouldn't be trying to ape a man but you would dress in tailored clothes. I was still wearing the suit my Dad's friend had made me, which was past its best. When I was stationed in the East End, along Cable Street was Max the tailor. I was on the beat one day and I saw that he'd got some half-made suits in the window like true tailors have. I peeked in the door. It wasn't every tailor made suits for women but he knew exactly what I wanted. He showed me one or two waiting to be picked up. So I had three of the most divine tailored suits I've ever had in my life, made by Mr Cohen. And he knew just what the very latest was because he made them for all the West End prostitutes who wanted the very best fashion – either one pleat at one side or two pleats or one button or two buttons or big lapels or short lapels. I had a beautiful black double-breasted barathea and a single-breasted hopsack in speckly lovat-green tweed, and a navy blue one. They cost a lot of money but they were worth it. He was some tailor.

I didn't have a lot of money but I always had a hat that was my favourite. Then when it got a bit too rough I'd buy another one from Scotts at the bottom of Bond Street. I had my hair long. I have only ever had it shortish twice. I'd wear it in a pile on the top under the hat.

You could get shirts made to measure in Hope Brothers at the end of the Strand going into the City or when I had the money Madeleine used to encourage me and we'd go into Burlington Arcade to order a shirt. She would have all the rolls of cloth brought out and we'd choose what colour I wanted. They were super. And you would have a tie that blended with it all and beautiful cuff-links, as flashy as possible, large coloured stones. You didn't just slop around.

And shoes, I used to buy brogues with little welts and beautiful stitching all round. They were quite expensive and if you paid another pound you could have them burnished. When you got them back you could see your face in them.

Madeleine and I did look a pair in all the gear. She was so proud of me looking butch. She'd say, "Now, have you got your big hand-kerchief? Have you got your money? Have you got your watch?" She was very loving and caring. A right little mother hen. You were really advertising yourself with your clothes and your hat and every-thing. Your partner would dress as smart as she could – what a woman would wear basically – but if she wanted to go a bit tailored it didn't matter. You didn't go out in wild gear. You'd just look a beautiful couple.

Although I was playing the butch role, if I felt, Oh I want to be a bit femmy tonight, I'd change my clothes to match my mood. Young people do today – they go out with all kinds of gear on just according to how they feel. So did we. In the police every so often you were issued with two white shirts and Madeleine jazzed up one of the discarded shirts for me with thick crocheted lace from the market. You couldn't buy a blouse like that during the war. So that was a very feminine shirt.

And you would always have a little finger ring on your left hand. That was one of the signs. If you were a lesbian, you wore a signet ring bigger and bolder and better than your next friend's ring. If somebody was out in the gear, you'd give them the glad eye, or they'd give you the glad eye. It was a bit difficult in the war years when so many were in uniform because they looked smashing and they all had shirts and ties. They all looked like lesbians and it wasn't so easily defined but when you saw the little finger ring you knew. If you were fixed up with somebody you'd also wear a wedding ring, third finger, right hand. Still wear mine, wouldn't come off now – beautiful wedding ring, worn so thin.

During the war a lot of women had trousers for their jobs and I began to wear trousers with my costumes. Because you could still look smart with trousers. You would have a lovely jacket that matched or a blazer-type thing. My favourites were checked, black and white checked.

Even after the war when I went into teacher training college, I screamed it because I was still wearing my costumes. I know a woman now, she's in her nineties and her friend is in her eighties and they've been together since they were young women. She still wears tailored clothes and shirts and ties. It's difficult when you get older – your neck goes like a turkey, scraggy thin neck. Unless you've got the money to have a shirt made, women's blouses are always somehow the wrong fit. Now you're lucky if you see a lesbian in a skirt. Most of them wear trousers, which I think is a shame really because when you've got lovely legs underneath why not show them off? Tights are a bit of a nuisance but stockings are very sexy with little black suspenders, and you get the fun of taking them off.

Butchy underwear used to be a man's vest and those woollen pant things like boxer shorts that are still fashionable today. But they were longer then with little legs and white, not fancy colours. I found them extremely comfortable underneath trousers, far more comfortable than knickers or panties – not just because they were menswear.

I liked tucking in my shirts because men's shirts were long and if you didn't tuck it in right, it was all bulky. You had to sort of wrap it round and tuck your hands right down each side, down the back, wrap the tails over. I used to kid myself when I was putting my trousers on. I do it from force of habit now. I never fasten them directly up the front. They're always put to one side. Sort of – "Which side do you dress?" – like the tailor asks you. To this day I always put them on one side.

It must have been pretty obvious that I was a lesbian. At one stage I remember going on an ordinary plain-clothes errand about some shop assistant that had disappeared from one of the big stores in Oxford Street. I got into the lift just as a man got in. He said, "Are you interested in making a bit of money? Without insulting you I think you've probably got a girlfriend, haven't you?" I said,

"Yes, I've got a girlfriend." He said "Well, I recognise a lesbian when I see one." All this in the lift! He said if we could put on a little show for him in his flat he'd give us quite a handsome sum of money because he'd like to see two lesbians making love.

"I'll give you my card."

But by then we were out of the lift. I said, "I don't think my friend will be interested, thank you," and shot off. But that was nothing unusual.

9

The Swarm and Swirl of Wartime

I was on Paddington Station the morning the war started. We were supervising the evacuation, seeing the little children and their teachers onto the trains. Off they were going to the countryside.

I wanted to be a pilot. I wanted to join the Air Force but I was in a reserved occupation – the police wouldn't release me. As the war progressed and many of the policemen were called up to fight, we were called on to do all the men's work. Other women would have been horrified to do some of the work we did. I learned about life, and the seamy side of life, too.

I remember conducting traffic in Leicester Square because the lights had gone wrong and the traffic was all jim-jammed together. There were a lot of big trucks that were collecting up rubble from the damage, and tanks and convoys of big lorries and forces passing through. I thought, oh I'll never do this. What is it you have to do? Oh yes, point decisively to the third one, tell him to stop. Horrifies me now to think about it. The traffic was completely in my hands. It gave me a feeling of power, of being important.

In the blackout you were supposed to stop when you stepped out the door and count to fifteen slowly to let your eyes adjust to the dark. As it was, the night would often be lit up with all the fires from the incendiaries. I'd be darting from one side of the street to the other to avoid the flames licking out of the buildings. I did once lose my way going to our flat because it was so thick with fog and smoke I couldn't find the front door.

We had sad duties with the war. You went to a bomb scene where there'd been a collapse of houses or flats and people distressed, running about or couldn't find their relatives and perhaps

A policewoman with evacuees.

•

they were there, dead, under the rubble. When I was stationed at Leman Street there was a big warehouse on Commercial Road. People whose homes had been destroyed could take refuge in there, sleep. It was very badly bombed in the Blitz one night. You can't describe the sound of a big, big building collapsing. It was somehow a different sound from a little house collapsing or going up in flames. Some American soldiers came and started at once, lifting by hand and crawling over the rubble. You could see a piece of something or somebody's bag and a limb or two and it was awful. As soon as the men saw us, two or three girls looking a bit green and being violently sick, they sent us off to another place where they were putting the bodies to see if we could help looking after the wounded.

It was life on a knife edge. You didn't know if you were going to be bombed next time, or even if you were going to come home when you went out. Now when I think, I don't know how I did it. It was pretty awful. People of my age now, we don't remember the horrors of it. Seeing a dead body or a few bodies with pieces off them lying about, you don't store it up. At the time you were filled with compassion or filled with horror. You had a good cry and then, next day, it all happened again and you stopped having a good cry, you took it. I suppose I was frightened, I can't think now. I don't remember shivering in my shoes. And I was young. You just thought – well, this is a war, get on with it. We didn't really have much time, too busy looking after other people, shepherding them into the shelters, helping people who had got lost, looking for some street or looking for some relative.

"Where are these houses? And when were they bombed? And where should we go? And how did it happen?"

You were so intent on helping in some way. It was afterwards when you got home or in the Tube going home, you wondered what it was all about. Why are we doing all this? But you went to bed and flopped and slept.

If you'd a bit of spare time you enjoyed it. You didn't sit around fretting. You were living on another plane. I can't say it wasn't exciting. You might not have liked some of the things you saw, but it was exciting because you never knew when you went out what you were going to come across. It was the swarm and swirl of wartime. The immediate future was unknown. You didn't plan for the future. You never said, "Well, when the war is over we'll do that, or we'll do the other." It was a long time before you started to think on those lines. There wasn't time to clear bomb sites and willow herb, that purply pink flower we called fireweed, covered up all the rubble. It didn't take long to grow. Some sites weren't cleared until well after the war.

I was on plain-clothes for quite some time with the beautiful Scots girl who'd carried me round the beat when I first started. The West End was full of little drinking clubs where all sorts of underhand things went on. One lot were printing ration books and stamps and forged passports. You'd have the runaway girls from home and you'd find the deserters there as well. Seedy little places. You just squashed in a little room in a basement. But they were always very respectful to me; they didn't know I was police. We were just a couple of friends that had come up to town.

We were looking for suspicious people and illegal immigrants as well. If you went round Soho you could always get a good meal at a Chinese restaurant if you kept your mouth shut about their cook or their kitchen hands. My friend Tonks badly wanted to come on plain-clothes duty as well but with her flaming red hair and pale skin she would really have been too conspicuous. There was a lot of following people round and making little notes and hiding behind here and there. See what time they came out and what they were wearing and who they came out with and what car they got in and what direction they went. Then when you'd done it a bit somebody else would take over because you hadn't to be noticed. Sometimes another police officer would have you in sight because something might happen to you.

And then I worked plain-clothes with JB, a man from the army, a Lieutenant-Colonel. For quite some time I worked with him and we became good friends. I don't know what he was doing. He never told me and I never questioned him. He did a lot of undercover work, a lot of secret work for the army. I would dress up and go out with him to high-class clubs and pretend to be his girlfriend. My mother made me a coat with twenty foxtails round the bottom so I would look the part. He knew I was a lesbian so there was never any hanky-panky. He used to give me pin-up magazines and say, "This might excite you, take it home." But we would spend the evening in the Kit-Kat Club or Murray's or the Embassy or the Hungarian, which was where the Duke of Windsor used to go, and behave like we were lovers. Can't think what he was looking for. He had big fish to fry. It was dangerous. I never quite knew if somebody was going to come up and shoot him. He told me who he wanted me to follow and chat up in the ladies room. Find out anything I could about them.

Another of the duties we had to do was escort German women to the Isle of Man. Under Defence Regulation 18B, German citizens who came to the attention of the authorities were detained for security reasons. We used to take the women over and I'd get friendly with them. Then when they knew the boat was coming in with the next lot, they'd come and bring me a posy of wild flowers, made specially. They used to make knickers from parachute silk, creamy colour or green or blue. They would put the two seams together and oversew them with silky cotton, very, very close and sometimes in another colour to give a thick ridge of silk line at the sides. They were beautifully made. We showed our friends how to do it afterwards. They used to do it because they were bored. They made a little business of it. I remember I had fabulous pyjamas made out of a pattern one of them had found in some old sewing book. There was one favourite I had on the Isle of Man. She had been a prostitute and she'd got that guttural accent which I found very fascinating. Beautiful legs and face with beautiful cheekbones. We would just hold hands and walk up round the hill or the island somewhere.

Every week I'd be picking up deserters from the street. They'd never been away from home before or they'd never been in groups before or perhaps they'd seen bombing near where they were and they were a bit scared. Sometimes they weren't even of age to be in the forces. They'd told the wrong age to get in. Nearly always they went home. Their parents would come for them. It wasn't quite what they thought it was going to be in the ATS or the WAAFs. If they were older girls, you'd ring up and they'd say, "Oh yes, she's listed as missing." So you'd take them to the station and the army would send somebody to take them back. I always felt very sorry for them. Sometimes they were very rude to begin with but

Barbara with her brother, Stanley, Euston Station, late 1940.

•

they just wanted somebody to tell it to, how awful it all was.

In 1941 my brother Stanley was killed – blown up on the HMS *Barham* in the Eastern Mediterranean. He was a wireless telegrapher. We had never been close because I was so busy when I was growing up. He was five years younger and he didn't want to come with his big sister. He wanted to be doing things with the lads.

When the war came along he joined the navy. He was thrilled. He used to write home and say, "This is the life for me, a life on the ocean waves." He loved it. He'd found his little niche with the right sort of fellas and the excitement. When the ship was hit they weren't even in battle. A torpedo came and just blew them up. I think there were three or four survivors out of the whole lot.

He'd just had his twenty-first birthday. You could send presents and parcels and because he was twenty-one my mother had made an enormous cake. She was famous for her fruit cakes. The cake and the inevitable socks that you always sent and two or three other things were stitched up in a piece of cloth with indelible ink on it. You didn't trust brown paper and string. That's how you had to pack a parcel going halfway around the world following a ship that you didn't know where it was. Anyway, the cruel thing was, six months after he was killed this parcel came back saying UNDE-LIVERED. You'd think they'd have chucked it into the sea, or dumped it.

His girl was just heartbroken. She was always a lovely little pianist but she shut the piano and said, "I'm not going to play anymore." She said she was joining the ATS, she was going to fight. She wanted to do her bit to the enemy. She was angry. Two years later I heard she'd walked into the Serpentine in the corporation park in Blackburn and drowned herself.

Barbara, 1946.

•

10

Words of Comfort

My queer friend, Cyril, was thrilled that I'd taken his advice and found somebody to love. I told him Madeleine and I were going to get married and were wondering where we could go for our honeymoon. Express came back: "Go to Jan and Bert's." Cyril said Jan and Bert would love us to go to their house for our honeymoon, to their little cottage in the country. This time we'd not had an engagement ring, just a wedding ring. Off we went to the church and we just knelt down, said a little prayer, all on our tod and off we went for our honeymoon to Jan and Bert's.

They made us a beautiful bed with all the best linen. Jan made wonderful food, which was a devil to get. Don't know where she scrounged it from but it was an absolute feast. She was running us round the countryside because by then Bert had a car. It was a wonderful week, just wonderful. Breakfast in bed, absolutely spoilt. It was heaven. They enjoyed it as much as we did.

Having seen Jan and Bert who divided up the ploys, we thought that was how all lesbians lived. That's how I thought it was going to be with Madeleine. I was visualising myself as taking the male part of the partnership. I would do the coals, bring them up from the cellar and I would do the painting, I would mend things and do the decorating. She would do the sewing, she would do the cooking. Very distinct roles. But it doesn't work like that. You find after a while that marriages are not like that. We both had a profession. We were both swotting for the sergeant's exam. Whoever was in the mood had to get up and get on with the cooking.

When things started to be in short supply, rationing was introduced. You only got two ounces of tea a week and at one point we were down to four fresh eggs a year. My mother's brother, Uncle Gilbert, sent food parcels from America, a lot of tinned things. A whole chicken in a tin once, that was stored for a long time because it was so precious. And he sent knickers, stockings, a pair of sling-back perspex shoes, diamanté earrings, a typewriter. If you went to anybody's house for a meal you would take them bits of rations, or you would take some coupons. There were canteens called British Restaurants so that you never needed to go hungry. You could always go in there and get a damn good meal for a shilling.

I grew vegetables, top of Notting Hill Gate. Four sisters had a big house with grounds. They went into the police station and said, "We've got all this ground, can we give you some to dig for Britain? Would some of your policemen like to turn it over?" You said if you wanted a piece and you went and plotted out your six by six. It was a lovely recreation to go up there and dig or stick in a few vegetable seeds. Someone would give you a few extras that they had, some little roots. Carrots were very popular. We grew spuds, Brussels sprouts and rhubarb. Madeleine used to put salted beans down and eggs down in isinglass. You could buy a little book for sixpence, *How to Preserve Your Fruit and Vegetables*. It was fun because you hadn't done it before. If you'd got something and you knew somebody else hadn't, you'd swap. It brought the best out in people.

Sometimes I might not see Madeleine for two or three days because I would be on night duty and she would be on a late turn or an early turn. On one occasion I'd come in from late turn, which meant getting home at eleven or twelve o'clock and she was in bed fast asleep. I was getting up early the next morning to be at work on the early turn. Instead of getting undressed in the bedroom I got undressed in the kitchen. I put all my clothes on a kitchen chair, ready to jump into in the morning. When I got up I couldn't see them and I thought, I'm sure I got undressed here last night. I woke up Madeleine and we were looking for this missing uniform and shoes. It was just as if I'd never put them there. I found my rain-coat had gone and my trilby hat so we realised then that we must have had burglars. How'd they got in? Where'd they gone out? When we looked in the lavatory there were some marks of some-body's toes down the wall. Somebody'd come in through the little tiny window that the cat used.

"I'll have to say I can't come to work, I haven't got my uniform. What's the time?"

When I looked at the mantlepiece, the clock had gone.

I went to the police box on the corner and said, "Sorry I'm late for work, but I think I've had burglars. Can you send a policeman?" Well, of course there were roars of laughter. We didn't live it down for months. Sometime later they arrested the bloke that had done our place over. In his flat were found bits of my uniform – the numbers from the lapels. He'd just sold it as a suit because people were desperate for clothes. They traced the clock to a pawnshop in Praed Street in Paddington. When we got it back it had the pawn-broker's marks on the back. We were ever so proud and used to show this clock to people.

Everyone was encouraged to do something extra for the war effort. Besides doing my police job, some evenings when I was on early turn I used to go to a little factory next to Portobello Baths where they made electric cable. It was monotonous and noisy. All I had to do was to feed grains and chips into a mincer and set all the buttons and then it would come out as flex. You'd to make sure it was winding itself slowly round the bobbins. I didn't get paid for it. That was my little effort for the war. Madeleine went regularly to a dairy farm just outside London to help the farmer with the animals.

It was a terrible time with the bombs. When you were saying goodbye to someone you never knew if you were going to see them again. Anxious times. We made a little rule with ourselves that you never went out and you never came in without saying or shouting,

"I've come home!" or, "Bye, I'm off now!" You always had a kiss when you came in, however tired you were and always had a kiss when you went out. You never went to bed with a cross word. If you had a few words, everything had to be settled and forgiven before you went to bed. I've tried to keep to that one because it's nice. We weren't on duty together. When one was home the other wasn't home. You'd think, God I hope she's going to come in tonight. So there was always that wonderful meeting when you did get home. Even if the other was in bed asleep and you crawled in bed next to her, it was never "Eurgh". It was always, "Oh, how wonderful to have you back," and a few words of comfort.

Often with things going wrong, people falling dead around you and having to do horrible things, I would write to my mother and say, "It was awful tonight" and you can bet your life next week she'd be up. With the warmth that she always gave she'd be comforting me. She'd be making me some little special food or seeing I got off to work. Only for two nights, perhaps, but she was always there if I wanted her. She probably would bring some fish, things that were rationed. She'd bring the sweets I always loved and chocolates. Often she'd find something new in the clothes line, nice piece of underwear. She always left a packet of postcards addressed with stamps. W0hen there was a bad raid in our part I just had to write "I am OK" on a card and drop it in the post.

Our landlord had little mattresses in the cellar of the house and my mother made siren suits for Madeleine and me in a fluffy woollen material. They were lovely and warm, like a boiler suit with a hood. When there were air raids on we'd wear them round the house in the evening. Then when we heard the siren we'd run down to the cellar and try to get some sleep there. It was fun. Mind you, when you really were faced with death and grief and homes destroyed that was just gruesome. That was heartbreaking.

11

On the Prowl

I was devoted to Madeleine. She was everything I'd wanted, my dream woman. But I broke her heart in the end. I was rotten. It wasn't entirely my fault though. I'd come from Blackburn where there wasn't another lesbian – that I knew of – and suddenly I was in London surrounded by policewomen. I think it went to my head. There was always someone running after me or wanting me to go to her room for a coffee. I often had a little flutter going on. I had a field day.

I had a lovely divertimento in Surrey. A woman had offered the police the use of a cottage in the grounds of her house, so four of us went down for the weekend – just to get away from all the bombing and all the sordidness. On the bus on the way down I was sitting next to one that I'd fallen for and kept giving her looks which she told me to stop doing. When I think now – I was a grown woman – I think how childish it was. I was wriggling about working myself up, because I was sitting next to her. Every time I looked at her I gave another little wriggle on the seat, got another little thrill, really working myself up. I felt her nearness. The things you get up to! I wanted her and she loved me but in a different sort of way. When she left the police force she met a woman from a completely different sphere of life and they've been together for fifty years. A lovely pair, still living together and I still go to see them.

Then on the odd occasion I'd been going off with a woman that Madeleine and I had met at the club in Mayfair. She was there with her partner. Her name was Jessie and she was a civil servant. I was living in the section house at Pembridge Square when we first started seeing each other. We had to meet when Madeleine wasn't there. It was all very complicated but all the more exciting of course, illicit lovemaking. There was only one door open when you came into the house at night. To come in with me Jessie had to get past a dragon of a woman sitting in a little office like a concierge, under the stairs, next to the scarves. She was there with her book to check you in and out. If you'd put on your application to be out till eleven o'clock and it was quarter past eleven she wanted to know why. Very strict about it all. You could have been lying dead somewhere, blown up. At one point Jessie had a broken leg but that didn't stop her, even with her leg in plaster. God knows how she did it. She had to slide past this woman on her bottom to keep out of view.

We used to go out like a couple of lads, for a night out, to enjoy ourselves at the cinema or a café or a show. Her partner and Madeleine would have a girly evening at home in one of the flats and we'd go off on the prowl. We really were a pair that egged each other on: "Oh go on, I dare you!" If you were in the Underground and you got a load of girls from the ATS, you bet your life some of them would be giving you the glad eye. And you could always get off, as they called it, if you wanted to. They'd look at you and then you'd look at them and you'd get a bit nearer and say, "Oh, have I seen you before? Where are you going tonight then? We're off to so-and-so, would you like to come with us?" We were all talk really. I don't think we would seriously have taken two girls off to a hotel. We certainly couldn't take them back to my place or Jessie's place but we weren't beyond sitting at the back row at the pictures. Being a policewoman, I always used to be saying, "Are you lost? Can I help you to find your way?" If somebody was standing, gazing around, I'd think, this is my opportunity.

Our partners began to suspect we were at it and not just going out to the theatre. They were furious. I remember we had been to see *Peer Gynt* and I used to go round the house singing Solveig's love song, and Madeleine thought there was something wrong in singing that. There was a bit of a flutter going on with Jessie at that stage. It was nothing serious. It would have fizzled out if we'd been left alone. But if somebody says "Don't!" to me, I shove my feet in and won't move, like a donkey. I just carried on with it which was very naughty because it did develop into quite a passionate affair. We went the whole hog.

Jessie was butch – not crude butch but definitely butch. Always looked funny dressed up in a skirt. Big shoulders and a good manly figure. She had lovely breasts: I always went for that. She had dimples when she smiled. And she nearly always had her hair cut short. I don't remember it ever being beyond a long man's cut. She'd go in the barbers to have it done. She always smelt nice and clean. She smelt a bit of shaving cream. And she liked to think that she was a tough.

We made love to each other – one up and one down and then swop over. That's what is so nice about lesbian relationships. You don't say to yourself, "Oh I'm a butch, she's a lovely feminine woman, I'm going after her." You might be two feminine-looking women, you might be two butch-looking women, but when you get stripped of your clothes, of the facade that you're walking about in, it doesn't matter. Maybe your femininity will come out in your love-making. Maybe the other side. You can follow your mood. Maybe you're in the midst of some affair and you're the dominant one. Then you see somebody else and think, I'd like her to do things to me – I'd like her to be the boss. Okay. Be all feminine. Put on your false eyelashes. Make up your face. Play the part.

Jessie used to love being almost naked and you'd to beat her. She'd take her belt off her trousers and she'd just lie there. She'd say, "Make marks, make marks on my bottom, I want to see marks when I look in the mirror." I never enjoyed it, never. But she'd say, "You don't love me if you don't do it." She never wanted to hit me, thank goodness. Sometimes she'd have collected a thin twig, like a willow and you'd think, God, this is going to hurt.

"Harder," she'd say, "harder, harder!" Never aroused me. It sounds like she was a bully but she wasn't aggressive. She wanted me to be aggressive to her.

She was a wonderful lover. She taught me a few things – she knew everything about sex. I didn't know much. That was part of the excitement in those days. You learnt a new trick. And the next person you were with, you passed on the new trick. She showed me how delightful a bath could be together. Never thought of that before. She taught me how sexy long hair can be when you're making love. You can do such beautiful things with long hair.

She had always wanted to find something that she could use for making love. You could buy them. They were called dildoes. But as she couldn't find one, she was darned well going to make one – to my horror. I don't know where she got the idea from but I was very angry about it. If I'd wanted that I'd have gone with a fella. I didn't want poking. But she used to get satisfaction wearing it in bed. She was very clever about it. She'd made it so that when she squeezed against it, milk would come out, warm milk. But I hated it, left me cold. It didn't last long that phase. She soon realised.

She was romantic as well. She loved magnolia buds. God knows where she pinched them from but as soon as the magnolia buds came through the door you thought, right I'm for it tonight. She used to say, "You're just like a magnolia bud and this is what I'm going to do to you," and do it to this bloody flower. I was crying out for it by the time she'd finished. After that I could never look at a magnolia bud without quivering.

It must have been Jessie who introduced me to oral sex. That's how naive I was. To me that was the ultimate of loving somebody, if you could make oral sex with them. Must love them a hell of a lot. To me that was the most you could do, the biggest thing you could do for or take from a woman. It was such an intimate private part – I mean you'd seen it, looked at it, and you'd kissed it, but to actually go all out with your mouth on somebody's intimate precious centre of them, it was a privilege that hadn't to be abused. You didn't abuse it. You had to bloody well mean it.

Of course, it came to a confrontation with Madeleine. You always get it at that age, until you're mature enough – "Choose her or me!" She could be a hot-tempered little spitfire when she was riled. But Madeleine didn't leave me. She waited a long, long time to see if I'd settle down.

12

A Period of Deep Sorrows

I was at Bow Street when the war in Europe ended. The Opera House was right opposite the police station. They changed the programme when they heard the news and put on *Sleeping Beauty*. At the end of our shift we went over in our uniforms. I remember we stood up at the back and everybody was so happy. It was a wonderful night. But no sooner had the war finished than a period of deep sorrows and unsettling events began. The next four years were to be a life in limbo for me.

That summer of 1945 my mother became really ill and I went home. By this time she and my father were running a little sweet shop. I took about two months off, special leave, to go home to nurse her. My sister, Midge, came up from Middlesex where she was teaching. My mother died of a broken heart. I do believe this is true. She had cancer, but she never would have had cancer, it wouldn't have got her if she had been normally healthy. Mothers have a special soft spot for sons and it just broke her heart when Stanley was killed. They took her to hospital and she tried to get better. The usual story. Walking round the street saying she was feeling better and everybody saying, "Oh, you're looking better." Of course, she wasn't.

She relapsed and was very ill. They brought her home then and Midge and my dad and I were taking turns at nursing her. At the end we'd to sit up all night with her. It was so hot. I remember we had the back door open to let air in because she couldn't breathe. It was cancer of the bowel. Those nights were terrible and my father, he was so sentimental and loved her so much, you could see him suffering. My mother was trying to be perky for our sakes and

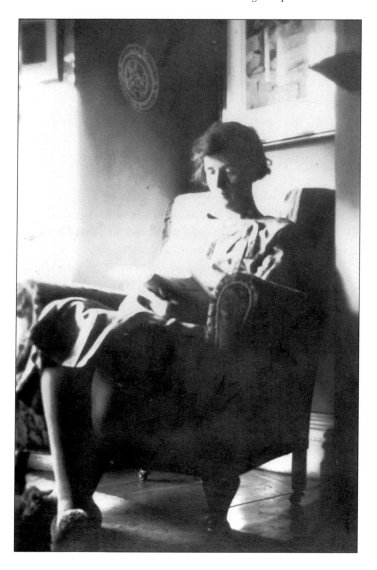

Barbara's mother, Beatrice.
●

we were putting it on for her sake. You'd think she was getting better. And then she'd try to walk or she'd try to sit up and then she'd be vomiting. Then she wouldn't be vomiting. You couldn't follow it.

It was too much, particularly for Midge. She was only a young girl. I was a bit experienced of life and I'd seen horrible things, but for Midge it was just terrible. She wasn't a person who could cry. If I have a sorrow everybody's to know about it and I cry and I cry and I cry till there's no more tears left in me. But Midge, when my mother died, she just got up from the chair, went and sat on the stairs and didn't speak to anybody for days. You spoke to her and she wouldn't speak to you. She just locked herself up. It was just one big sadness.

All the people of our district knew and loved my mother because she was always helping others. After she'd died, people used to stop me in the street and tell me what she'd done for them. She was the rock of our family. She was the foundation. My brother had gone and now she'd gone. Poor old Joe was desolate, stunned by it all. What should we do with Joe? What should we do with Midge? I then had to go back to work. Go back to London.

Midge went back to her teaching job in Middlesex. She was twenty-one and she'd not long taken up with a woman in the police. They were living together in West Kensington. My dad sold up everything in Blackburn and came to London as well. Madeleine and I got a flat for him opposite ours. He worked in a greengrocer's shop and he liked that, meeting people. But he didn't have a life. He was a stranger in a foreign land. He missed his brother and he missed his few relatives and friends and he decided he'd go back to Blackburn. Maybe I should have looked after him more and given him more but I had made my life separate from home. We bought back the sweet shop in Blackburn and he bought a little house nearby.

One morning, it was almost a year to the day after my mother had died, my dad didn't turn up at the shop. The people next door heard the dog barking and saw the dog in the yard so they called the police. They broke in and it looked as if he had had some kind of a stroke. He'd slipped behind the kitchen door so he was shut in the kitchen. It was only a little scullery kitchen, little tiny house. The tiniest jet on the cooker was on but not lit although his porridge was still in the pan and the water boiled away. Well, when they told me I was on duty, Bow Street, and it was evening. They sent for me and just blithely said, "Your father's had an accident, he's dead and you've got to go home at once."

There was an inquest. It didn't cross my mind that he might have committed suicide until they gave the open verdict. I don't think, however unhappy he was, he would have had the courage to end his life. Certainly not in that slow tortuous manner. That's what gets me. I think he was just so distressed he didn't know what he was doing. It was his custom to put the porridge on all night in a double saucepan with a tiny light. Little tiny light it was. He'd have opened the door to let his dog out in the backyard, that was the first thing he did every morning. No doubt, the draught blew the light out – the little tiny light – and the gas was leaking. That's what I feel.

My father's brother, who was a minister, came to take the service and to bury him. He was buried with my mother outside Blackburn in a little cemetery called Feniscliffe. Anyway, it was a relief for him. In a way I was glad because he was very unhappy, very miserable. I don't think he would have got over my mother's death. He'd lost his son as well. He'd lost his daughters. We'd gone away. We'd fled. We weren't living like a lot of other people's children, at the other end of the town or two streets away. We'd gone. We were lost.

I got extended leave and stayed in Blackburn. When I'd been up there a few weeks I decided to leave the police. I'd been made a sergeant and was studying to become an inspector, which I wasn't finding easy. If I'd sat my exam and not passed I don't think I could have stood it. My inspector encouraged me to leave. She was very envious of me in more ways than one – envious of my relationships and of my commendations.

Joe had left the little shop to Midge and me. There was only us two girls. Midge had no desire to come back and vegetate in Blackburn so it was suggested that Jessie would buy her out. So Jessie left the civil service, which I suppose was her way of showing that she really loved me and wanted to be with me.

Poor Madeleine was being pushed more and more into the background and of course was heartbroken that she wasn't asked to come or that I didn't come back to her. She was more than ready to take me back. I think I saw this as a way of getting off the hook. I don't know why because she was a perfect little wife and wonderful partner in every way.

There have been times in my life when I've been a rotten thing, when I've got somebody great, some smashing woman and then somebody's waved a little finger and said, "Come on, I like you," and I've given in to temptation. Then I've got enmeshed in all the pain and jealousy – I've felt that I'm in a net and I must get out. To break free from the situation, I've broken free from the woman I was with, even though it might not have been the right thing to do.

Madeleine is one of the people that I really hurt, really and truly hurt because I'm sure she was ready to go through life with me and I could have done a lot worse than having her, a lot worse. It was a long, long time before she looked at anybody or anything. Eventually she got married – the fella with the dairy farm where she'd been helping out in the war.

So Jessie and I were living in Blackburn and running this shop. Well, two people couldn't live on a little shop like that. We couldn't survive. We talked it over and I thought I would go and try to be a mannequin since I'd really wanted to be a model when I'd had the offer of training years before. So I wrote off to Manchester, which was our nearest school and they took me on. I went to this school for several weeks and my God, it was a good training. I've got my

Barbara as a mannequin.

•

certificate to this day. I got an X certificate, which meant excellent. If you were Lucie Clayton trained, well, you were top school. I hawked this certificate around and got quite a lot of freelance jobs.

I loved the work. I kept all the programmes for a long time. It said what you were wearing and what was being shown and it gave the name, 'Mannequin, Barbara Bell'. It was very different in those days. You didn't dance on like they do today. You had to do the correct turns and the correct sitting down and getting up, the correct way to take your coat off and no trailing it on the floor behind you like they do now, all casual. I love that *Clothes Show* that they do on TV. It's about the one programme I watch.

Poor Jessie, of course, was stuck home in the shop, whilst I was going off, early morning train to go to Manchester or going off early evening for some evening show. We didn't know anybody, didn't know any girls. I felt too ashamed to contact Jan and Bert because I'd gone back with somebody else. Cyril came a few times but he came on his own – most of the boys had gone off doing things during the war.

There was no social life. It was a disaster after you had been in the swirl of the pool of London to come to these still waters. Oh, it was a nightmare! If you went to the cinema it was something that had been shown about two years before in London. And the clothes looked so antique. So we decided we'd pack it up and sell up. We weren't there that long, perhaps a year, maybe less. Both of us realised it was a complete and utter disaster. We sold up and went back to London.

13

Another Door Opens

Jessie and I rented a house on Clapham Common. It was an awful place, a dilapidated, bombed house that had never been repaired. We got it as a stopgap really. The landlord was a Dutchman who was a villain. When it rained there was water streaming down one wall.

Neither of us had got a job. Jessie was fretting because she was a hard-working person and hated being idle. The army had sent a big force over to Europe to keep an eye on the Germans after the war – to oversee the disarmament process. Jessie joined up and was posted to the British Army of the Rhine. She loved the uniform.

It was time for our relationship to end. We didn't try to keep it up. But then, laugh your head off, who do I give her an introduction to but Trudi. I said, "If you're ever near, go and look her up and see if she wants something. See if you can do anything for the family." So she became real friends with them. Used to take them coffee beans from the NAAFI. Got little Dresden bits back in exchange. And then, of course, the inevitable happened: she and Trudi fell in love.

Later on, when Jessie came home on leave she brought Trudi with her. Well, I hadn't seen Trudi for years and years. I think it was the worst ordeal of all my life to see these two ex-lovers together. To see my first love as a grown woman, still very beautiful and speaking with Jessie as a lover. I wanted to run and hug Trudi and squeeze her and say, "I'm sorry for all I've felt, all these horrible things about you." But I had to restrain myself. I realised then that I still loved the woman because of what she had meant to me when I was growing up. We'd had the first experiments of lovemaking together so she was very special. And then there was Jessie who had given up her career to come and live with me in the North — must have loved me to do that. It was just a turmoil inside me. I wept for days after they'd gone.

Jessie was a mistake, but in spite of being a mistake, for years and years, and years and years, that woman sent me roses every birthday. Red roses in a box about three feet long. There was a note inside telling you how to care for them when you got them. Cut two inches off the stems and lay them in a bath of water for two or three hours, leaves and flowers. I've always done that with roses, ever since. It was romantic. No message, just the roses. For years those came, even when she was in Germany. I don't know where she is now. I lost touch with her but she eventually 'married'. She went back into the civil service somewhere up north and made a home with one of the telephonists.

After Jessie had gone I tried to get modelling work but it was a hard struggle. I dolled myself up and trailed all round Wimpole Street where all the fashion houses are. It was different from the work I'd been doing in Manchester and Southport where you just went for some show. In London the house took you on and you were their model. It was very difficult to crash into this market. I was thirty-three. If you were freelance you didn't stand a chance at that age. I did get a few jobs but I thought, this isn't the life for me. And the fellas were always after you, they were a bore.

I shouldn't have left the police — that's one of the mistakes in life I admit to. After the war the women's police force began to take off. All my companions worked their way up and got really good jobs. They went up in leaps and bounds.

So then I was floating. I'd lost my career. I'd lost my lover. I'd lost my flat. My three ambitions were gone. I missed my Dad. I missed my Mum like hell because she wasn't there to give me advice or to listen to my worries. I missed her encouragement and her protective love. But in these limbo years I remembered her

Barbara with her father's dog, Rufus, 1947.

philosophy that when one door shuts another opens. I was sure something would turn up when it was time.

I decided to live on my savings for a while and the proceeds from my Dad's house and shop. Tonks, my very dear friend from the police, filled the gap left by Jessie and Madeleine. We were never lovers but she was a wonderful friend, she still is. She could see that I was very unhappy in the house at Clapham Common. She was encouraging me to look for somewhere else but I felt too washed out.

While she was there one day, when I was just at rock bottom, the post came. There was a letter telling me that my name had now come to the top of the list for a flat with the Women's Pioneer Housing Scheme. They were a women's co-operative that I'd come across in the course of my work as a police officer. They bought houses and converted them into accommodation for distressed gentlewomen. Although I hadn't needed anywhere at the time, I thought I might be grateful of a place when I was old. So I'd bought up ten shares at a pound apiece and become a member. I must have been on their list for four or five years at least and I'd forgotten all about them.

The letter had been following me from pillar to post. It said reply within two weeks and this must have been well over two months. Tonks said, "Come on, get in a taxi. We can't spare a moment." I was so anxious to get out of this foul place in Clapham. The housing association office was in Buckingham Palace Road. The flat they'd written to me about had gone but they offered me another one in Redcliffe Gardens near Earl's Court where quite a lot of queers lived.

I began to live again when I got into that flat. It was top floor – it had a sloping ceiling and a dormer window – there was a funny kitchen and a bathroom that was shared with the flat at the front of the house. The bathroom was over the stairwell, between the two flats and opened into both of them so you had to remember to bolt both doors. To be able to make a home again was paradise, even on my own. It was the first time in my life that I wasn't sharing with anybody and I felt it was my private place, cosy and safe.

Shortly after I moved in, Midge and I decided it was time to keep a promise we'd made to our mother. Not long before her death she'd given us some money she'd put aside for us to go and visit her brother in America. We'd dreamt of going ever since we were little girls when Uncle Gilbert had sent us each a dollar to buy boots for school and a dollar at Christmas to buy what we wanted. It was quite a lot of money then so we were quite fond of this uncle we'd never seen.

We had to be the tops for this trip. We went to Harrods to buy coats. I got a hat with grapes all round the crown and Midge got a clochey sort of hat. We paid a fortune for these clothes because we didn't want to let the side down. We did it all first class – flew there and came back on the Queen Mary. I hoped the trip would help bring Midge out of herself.

Our uncle took us all round the East of America and into Canada. We had to see New York and Washington and all the sights. It was an adventure. We went to Niagara Falls and walked underneath, dressed in peculiar waterproof garments like road menders' outfits. We went to barbecues where they'd give you a whole sirloin steak as big as a man's hand – and expect you to eat it. We went to supermarkets – which we'd never seen before – and department stores and saw food we could scarcely believe. We saw feminine underwear in lovely colours, with hearts on and 'I love you' – we thought they were outrageous. We were used to utility clothing, austerity and scarcity – rationing lasted well after the war in England.

Every day there was a new something to see. We went for a trip to the Adirondack Mountains. It seemed a wilderness to us. We stopped at a wooden shack and ordered tea and we were given a cup of hot water with a tea bag in the saucer. We said, "Where's

Barbara (right) with her sister, Midge, setting off for America.

the teapot? Where's the tea leaves?" We'd never seen a tea bag.

We were driven round Harlem which was a revelation to my sister and me. Growing up, we'd hardly seen any black people – in fact, as children we used to be threatened if we misbehaved: "I'll bring the black man to you." In America we often saw 'No dogs, no negroes' on shops and hotels so the black people were classed along with dogs. I would have loved to have got out and had a good gossip with them because I was that sort of person. But we never got out of the car – we didn't know Uncle Gilbert well enough to ask. It was obvious you didn't associate. Riding round New York in trams, we soon found out that black people stood at the back while white people sat at the front. I was shocked but I saw this was how everybody behaved. I think it's terrible now.

A lot of Uncle Gilbert's friends were Lancashire people and they'd want us to speak dialect to them so Midge and I went into really broad Lancashire, "Go bang thy head on slopstone" and they roared about laughing. We were special – we were among the first English people to visit that part of America after the war and they thought we were heroines to come though all those air raids – they looked at us for scars! And the fact that I'd been a policewoman in it, well, that was very special.

They were very interested in what was going on in England to get the country back on its feet. Being a teacher, my sister was bleating on about this wonderful scheme we had for training teachers because there was a great shortage – short-term, intensive training. Emergency Teacher Training it was called. It dawned on me that maybe this was something I could do. As soon as we got back to England, I applied.

14

Drawn into a Dark Tunnel

Our trip to America did us both the world of good. It was two years since my Dad's death and Midge seemed to be over the worst. She was teaching at Fulham Central School in London. She was living with a policewoman called Jo Mitchell that she'd met through a friend of mine. Jo had more or less seduced Midge. Midge had had little affairs with girls at school and she had had boyfriends but nothing serious – we didn't in those days. I wasn't surprised that she'd become a lesbian – everything her sister did was right, follow her sister. Midge absolutely adored Jo. I think she was a mother figure as well as a lover. Midge was very happy there for two or three years. But she was beginning to spread her wings and do other things like joining dancing clubs and going with gangs of girls – not because she didn't love Jo but because she was young. Jo was older than Midge; she'd done all these things. She was jealous and in the end she picked up with another woman.

On the top of the bus on her way to work one morning Midge took an overdose. They brought her home from the school. I was just horrified: I didn't know she had been so deep into the relationship with Jo. And she was still harbouring guilt about my father, felt she should have gone back to Blackburn with him. It was very scarifying for me because I'd never come across any mental illness close to me. I really didn't know how to cope. I called the doctor and he said there was a danger that Midge was either going to harm me or harm herself and she must go to the detention ward of Fulham hospital. He called in the police and another doctor – there had to be two. They said when she came out they would arrange treatment for her. I was heartbroken, I thought this was a terrible thing to do to my sister, but they persuaded me that this was the only thing that might help her. I've always had a simplistic faith in doctors – if I've been recommended to do something by a doctor I've thought that must be the right thing.

I went with Tonks to see her. It was a terrible place – everybody shouting and screaming. We'd to look through some bloody wire netting to talk to her. She was locked in. They'd taken her two false teeth and her glasses and given her a garment – an awful cotton Magyar thing, round neck and plain sleeves. Her hair was all scruffed up. I said to Tonks, "I can't see her like this." And yet in a way I'd put her there – I'd said to the doctors, "Yes."

Midge was saying, "I want to come out," so we made an appointment to see the superintendent. I had to go before a board. I was shattered when they said, "Oh, you can't take her away, she's here for a month now at least. She's in the middle of her treatment. If you take her out now you'll regret it." What a terrible thing to say to somebody! I said, "I'm sorry, I've got to." They said, "Well, you will have to sign that you're responsible for her and for her actions." Which I did. It was a very difficult situation for me. I didn't know if I was doing the right thing for her. I can't bear to see suffering of anybody I love. I loved this girl and I didn't know if she was going to get better in my care.

She came to live with me in my flat in Earl's Court. It was one of the very unhappy times of my life. I wept. I wept buckets. I had never had a sleeping pill in my life, but the doctor said, "You have to have a good night's sleep," and he gave me one pill. I'll never forget that horrible feeling of being drawn into a dark tunnel. I tried to crawl out but I couldn't. And there was Tonks stroking my face and saying, "Now, it's going to be all right, I'm here with you. I'm looking after Midge, go to sleep, you're all right." I remember as if she was saying it yesterday. She was a wonderful friend.

Midge agreed to go for treatment with a psychologist. We were very lucky to get him. She went for quite a few months. I went with her the first couple of times and then he said she'd to come on her own. Then he said she'd to stop telling me what had happened. She also had a full course of electric shock treatment at St Thomas' Hospital, which she says saved her from madness. The treatment made her very dopey and it was awful for her on the Underground coming home because people would think she was drunk.

I used to be literally praying when Midge was out that she would get back safely. I thought anything might happen to her – she might throw herself under a bus or be a bit fey and walk off somewhere and forget where she was. If she went to the lavatory I was glad when she came out again. But I felt I'd betrayed her. She never held it against me, bless her. She got over it. But she didn't have any more lesbian affairs after that. When she was well she went back to teaching.

Tonks was quietly practical. She never blew up and never rushed, just sustained motion all the time. I leaned on her a lot. We had both applied for the emergency teaching course and been accepted. We had to wait three months before the course began so what were we going to do in this three months? Tonks said, "Let's go to France. We'll do the youth hostels, hitchhiking and a little train hopping." Midge was on the mend by now so I felt it would be all right to go.

Great planning went into it. We used to practise on Sundays, carrying a haversack with heavy tins all round Earl's Court to get us toughened up. I made some travelling clothes, beautiful cream flannel culottes and a bush jacket with stitches that could easily be unpicked. The idea was that when we got into a hot climate, we undid the stitches, took the legs off, took the sleeves out completely and finished with shorts and blouson. We looked damn smart. We bought little paper knickers from Dorothy Perkins. You could just chuck them away, they were wonderful for travelling, quite cheap.

Tonks invented trolleys for our haversacks, a walking stick and two wheels. Very, very good they were. And so the time came for us to leave. We went to Victoria station and were running at the last minute down the platform and this damn trolley of hers collapsed. We roared. She had to chuck it away – mine lasted quite a long time.

We went all through France. We'd decided we'd go to a place called Barcelonnette where there was a hut halfway up a little mountain. When we started asking around local people, they looked at us like we were mad and of course we were – going through the Alps in the middle of February. On foot. In the snow! It was impossible to get to this hut even with guides so we decided to go south.

We got all kinds of peculiar hitches on carts and bicycles. That was the first time I saw mimosa growing, with snow. It was out of this world. We went down to Grasse on the Riviera and Nice, to a wonderful youth hostel on a hill through lanes all smelling of orange blossom.

When we were almost at the Italian border we thought, why don't we go into Italy? And so we did. Well, that was the best experience of the whole trip. Got on a bus and the only thing the customs wanted to know was had we got any bananas! We went into a medieval town called Lavagna along the Italian Riviera to change some money. The bank manager was one of those swift little Italians and when he knew we were English he said, "Are you free this afternoon? Will you permit me to show you my beautiful Italian coast?" He spoke very precise English, self-taught Jane Austen English.

Oh, we thought that would be lovely. So he turned round and announced to the bank that he would be closing in half an hour so they could all have a holiday – the English girls were in town. We were in the square at the appointed hour and this little man in his long overcoat came bristling along. He'd brought out a carriage from where it'd been put for the war. The fringe was all rotten and the horse looked like it was going to collapse any minute. He dusted it out and took us along the coast. His name was Mr Carbone and that was the beginning of a lifelong friendship.

Tonks and I had a most wonderful tour of Italy. In Rome we slept in a youth hostel underneath the big stadium that Mussolini had built and then we went to Venice and on to Capri. We had a good two months of it.

Because of the war things hadn't really got in motion again. Everything was still in upheaval. We heard people's stories – how they had suffered and how they had nothing. They'd buy anything, buy your toothbrush or a bit of string. We set up by the side of the street, selling our last bits to make some money to get home.

15

I Quite Liked Being Worshipped

My first teaching job was in Shepherd's Bush, a real tough school. It nearly killed me at first. I specialised in Housecraft and preparing all the lessons was awful. I used to cry. Midge helped me: she used to write out the bloomin' recipe cards. She'd say, "Oh, you'll be all right after a year," because you were on probation for a year. I thought it was dreadful. However I got through my probation and then began to love it.

The Housecraft room was in a big hut with a tin roof and wooden beams – everything echoed. The children were real little toughies, walking about with tea cosies on their heads when they were making the tea and larking about. Everybody thought they were quite out of order. I don't know if it was my police training and my police discipline but I just had that little extra authority about me that won them over. If they were naughty, I used to say, "I'll ask you to do something and, if you don't do it, I'll tell you to. And if you still don't do it, and I think it has to be done, I'll make you do it." They soon cottoned on.

But I had a hankering to get into approved school work. One of my police duties had been to escort girls to Home Office approved schools and I used to think, whatever happens to them when we've gone? So when I saw a job advertised in the educational supplement I applied. What a cheek I had, it was for a deputy headmistress and I'd only been teaching for a year and a half. But I easily got into it with my police experience. It was with the London Police Court Mission at one of their schools just outside Watford – Delrow House.

I had been there a month only, and the head came in one day

and casually said, "You can manage now, I'm off for two weeks' holiday, you get on with it." I was chucked into running this place. The girls were mostly scruffy, very young – eleven, twelve onwards – sent there by the court because they were beyond parental control. Sex was often involved in it somewhere. They were just men-crazy some of them. We actually had a nurse on duty to tend to their VD every day. They were little thieves as well but I immediately fell in love with all these girls. I thought what a wonderful load of kids they were because they were little fighters. Made me reassess my values. I used to think it was their parents should be there, not them. Of course, with my police background, to them I was a 'pig'.

On a summer evening, you'd hear a roar of a motorbike and you'd think, oh God, another one got out! They'd go down the fire escape and get on the fella's motorbike that was waiting for them, all in their nighties and go off and have a bit. You never knew which one had been out, you just heard the motorbike and there were loads of giggles next morning. The other staff said, "You used to be a policewoman, what can we do?" So I said, "First thing, shall we have some alarms on the windows?" Whilst we were waiting for these alarms to be fitted we tried putting cocoa powder on the fire escapes. Next morning there'd be cocoa on the sheet and you'd know – it's that little devil that's been out.

If they ran away there was a great panic because it was such a disgrace to you as headmistress. Anybody with a car was sent out and if you hadn't a car you were on a bike. You had to leg it all round the country lanes looking for them and alert the local police stations. You'd to catch them if you could, bring them back – woe betide you if you didn't catch them.

There was a biggish teacher there with a big bosom. She made a beeline for me and I soon realised she was a lesbian. I'd never had a woman with bosoms that big before. Hers were like footballs. It was agreed she would come to my room and we would have some lovemaking. Mind you, all the doors were locked when you went to bed, so if anybody was visiting you, they had to unlock their door, lock it behind them, quietly creep along, come in and lock your door – all cloak-and-dagger. But when we were undressed in bed I was quite put off with these great big boobs. They were all round my head, I felt suffocated. Really put me off big bosoms for ever. She was a lovely person. For a very long time I kept a gold tiepin she brought me. That was the only flutter I had there.

When I'd been at Delrow House for two years, I wanted a change and I went to a school run by the National Association for Mental Health. The headmistress wasn't slap-dash, happy-go-lucky, like the other one. She was very intellectual and very proper, an Oxford graduate. Every girl that came to this school volunteered to come. She was given the option to be shut up in some sort of borstal or come to this open school and agree to take treatment. Although they were in for theft or burglary or masterminding some raid they also had some mental disturbance. They were very clever girls, mostly, and beautiful – sophisticated young women.

The school was on the outskirts of Staines, a Queen-Anne house in its own grounds. You could walk through the gates – they were always open, beautiful big iron gates – up the drive and see people walking about. And when we went out, they were never in croco-dile or uniform like these other kids had been. The dressmaking teacher used to buy dresses, coats, shoes at the Harrods sale. When a girl came in, she was taken to choose her wardrobe – it gave her a feeling of dignity and importance. So when they went out they looked like an academy for young ladies.

If one of the girls became very disturbed she would be given drugs and put into a coma. It was called Deep Sleep Therapy. She'd say goodbye to everybody, put all her little bits in a case and go up to the attic with the psychiatric worker. She would stay up there for a week and sleep and come down again smiling and calm.

I loved approved school work and I loved the girls but it was extremely tiring. In my time off I tried to refresh myself and refill myself with calm things and cultured things so that I could go on a bit longer. I was close to a woman called Emily Packer, a lecturer I'd met on the emergency teacher training course. She helped and advised me and I visited her in Sussex whenever I could.

I started taking refuge from work by frequently going to Italy to stay with Mr Carbone and his mother and his sister, in Chiavari. I did all sorts of things to make money for these trips. My sister, Midge, had come to live in the Redcliffe Gardens house by then. We were not far from the football ground at Fulham. When a big match was on I'd look round the flat and say, "What have we got we can sell?" One time it was a big old wireless.

"We'll write a label, FOR SALE. What do you think it's worth? Ten pounds we need this week," – that was a lot of money.

So when they were all coming out from the match, there was Midge with this wireless for sale. And then we took in a fella who was at the Earl's Court exhibition – he could have been anybody! Midge stood outside with a ROOM TO LET sign. So we both had money to go away.

I really needed my trips to Chiavari. I'd fly out to Italy from Gatwick, which was then quite a tiny airport. I went dozens and dozens of times. I never took anybody with me because this was my domain, this was my haven. They were lovely people. I loved Mami and I used to read to her – no idea what I was reading. I'd got very little chance to practise my Italian. I went walks with Mami to the sea, she'd come with me to see me swim. She was a sweet old thing.

They had a house in a grand square with an enormous garden. It had four huge front doors – one front door you went into and up a beautiful marble staircase. The central hall had paintings on the ceiling of Queen Isabella with Christopher Columbus bringing the first slaves to her. I had a big bedroom on the second floor with a cardinal's bed that you had to almost climb into.

One night, I woke up with a feeling of a presence in the room – that there was something or somebody there. I couldn't hear a

Barbara at the *lavatoria* at the Carbone house.

sound and it was pitch-black with the shutters closed. Eventually there was a little sigh. I said, "Who's there? There's somebody in my room. Who is it?" Cross by this time. From somewhere in the darkness came Mr Carbone's voice, "Ssh, Donna Barbara! It's only me, Emanuelo. Don't disturb yourself, go to sleep. I'm here to worship you." I could just make him out, kneeling at the foot of this big bed as if in prayer. I said, "What do you mean, you're worshipping me? Do you want to get into bed, is that what you're after?" He said, "Oh, never, never! No, no!" The next day he said he was sorry he'd disturbed me and he hoped he hadn't upset me.

It was rather nice, really. I like the sort of men that aren't wanting to paw me or have me jump into bed with them or make them a good meal or mend their clothes or go and clean for them. Oh no, he'd to cook for me! I wasn't allowed in the kitchen for years because it was beneath me. I was never allowed to dirty my fingers. He didn't come into my room again – as far as I know – but later he converted some of the servants' quarters into a flat for me. For many years this was Donna Barbara's flat. I was underneath his room then and he would lower things down. There would be a little basket swinging outside my window in the early morning with a single rose sitting in it. Another morning it would be a couple of figs on some leaves or a peach. I quite liked being worshipped.

Mr Carbone was a highly intelligent man, highly gifted. I learnt a lot from him. He used to take me out to the mountains, digging up all kinds of minerals and fossils and telling me what they were. He immediately recognised I was a lesbian but he never really used to speak openly about it. He would speak about what the homosexuals had done in Italy as film directors and artists and musicians, always in praise of them. He was never, as far as I could tell, a homosexual himself – he was just a neutral. He was always asking me to marry him – he thought we'd make a good team. I just used to laugh.

I loved his sister Syria. Syria loved me. We had a very deep relationship. She didn't speak English and I only speak a little Italian. We used to have a little cuddle or a kiss but that was all. She wasn't an active lesbian, I think she never had a boyfriend because her brother didn't approve – thought he might lose his best servant if she went off. He was a very selfish man, generous but selfish, you can be the two. He wanted his sister to be always there, she'd always to be the hostess.

Syria had a friend, Gina, who was definitely a lesbian – we clicked immediately. Nothing was said, but she knew and I knew. She was an artist and she looked like an attractive young boy. She used to come with us on picnics when we drove up through the olive groves to some mountain village. Then we were invited to her family for sumptuous meals in the garden, in bowers of vines with grapes hanging all round. She used to light candles in the evening. I think she was fond of Syria but she wasn't able to do anything about it – I think she'd have been drummed out of the village if they thought she was living with a girlfriend. She would come to the house in the early morning and shout up at the window to Syria. She'd be carrying a big lily or a beautiful rose – a bit like Mr Carbone did with me.

Much later on a homosexual friend of Mr Carbone told me there was a lesbian club in the neighbouring town of Lavagna but I never went. The Carbones were very well known and respected in the town. I think they wouldn't have liked it – I wouldn't have offended them for the world.

And now Syria's died, Mami's died, Mr Carbone's died and their home's been preserved as a museum. It's sad when a family dies out like that. They did mean a lot to me. I was an adopted daughter really.

Sometimes on these trips I would stop off in Paris to go to Le Monocle. During the war I'd become very friendly with one of the Paris police chiefs who was doing undercover work with JB. His son invited me to stay with him and his wife. They helped me to find Le Monocle again. I think it was nostalgia, wanting to see it again because I'd been so happy there with Trudi.

I was sitting on my own at the bar when a young woman came and sat next to me, very feminine. She was working there as a hostess. The bar woman introduced us. I told her I'd visited the club before the war and we got talking. Then she said, "Would you like to come upstairs with me?" She asked the madam — "That's all right," — so she took me upstairs to a little room with a big bed. Round the walls and over the door were heavy curled curtains. There was a table and chairs and a chaise longue. We chatted for a long time and then we had a drink and then we made love. You could have your drinks brought up and when you left you paid the madam for the drinks and the girl.

I'd never paid for sex before — it made the experience more thrilling. It was just an experiment, a big adventure. It wasn't sheer lust, "I must have a woman, I'm going to pay for it." Nothing of that sort. You didn't have to do anything, the girl just came to you or the madam would ask you if you wanted a partner. You could choose a butchy one or a femmy one. You could just go up with somebody you got off with at the bar as well — if you were a fast pair.

I liked that young woman very much. She said could she see me next morning so we had coffee together in a little café and she told me a bit of her life story. I gave her my petticoat because she'd admired it so much — wrapped it up in a parcel for her. It was crepe de Chine, accordion pleated, shocking pink. In the club I'd been wearing my black silk suit with a very tight-fitting skirt. The petticoat fitted, slinky underneath but when I sat down at the bar it made a burst of shocking pink across my legs. I loved that petticoat. So did she. She was very happy to have it. I only ever saw her the once.

16

Brahms Did the Trick!

After about three or four years of doing approved school work I was worn out, because you were just giving, giving, giving, all the time. Although I still had my flat in London, I hardly got to the damn place. It was such intense work and I always seemed to be on duty. I'd very little time for a social life and there was nobody there I really liked anyway – well, I liked them all but there was nobody caught my eye. The Home Office were then very short of head-teachers and two or three times they tried to persuade me to take a headship – not a headship round the corner in Earl's Court Road, or the centre of somewhere: it was Scotland or down in Devon. I thought, oh no, I can't possibly. But I was getting very tired. I decided then that I must make up my mind to either devote my whole life to this work, which was a work of sacrifice really or go back to ordinary teaching. I decided that I must have a rest from it.

I moved to Patcham, near Brighton in Sussex to live with Emily Packer, the lecturer I'd met on the emergency teacher training. I'd had my antennae out from the start of the course because I'd been without a partner since Jessie'd left. Emily was the science mistress. She'd stood up, she'd said, "I teach you about living things." I'd thought, ooh God, that's what I'd like to know about, Living Things. She commanded respect, as a lecturer, no monkeying about with her. If you came in a bit late, you had to make a speech saying, "May I join the class please?" You didn't just slink to your seat. And people loved her for it.

Tonks had been accepted on the same course and she made a beeline for another lecturer. Although we were mature students, we used to do silly things, like girls do at school, spending our sweet ration, and leaving chocolate on their desks.

"Oh, these are very nice, now who knows I like Mars?"

I was so attracted to her. I thought, I want to know her better. But I didn't know if she was a lesbian or not. I didn't want to offend her or embarrass her. I was merely a student so she was very superior to me. She was above reproach – above approach.

I began by waiting for Emily when she was coming out and asking which tram she was going on, telling her about my flat. If she'd like to escape from living in the college, would she like to come? Yes, she'd like to come. I cooked her nice little dishes and we talked. I learned that she had a strong relationship with another teacher called Meg. They'd met on their first teaching job and remained friends ever since. They were partners in crime, more or less. They used to go off on holidays and visit each other all the time but their jobs took them to different parts. It was always understood that when they retired they would live together. Emily was only about forty at this time so that seemed like a very distant prospect.

I decided it was safe to make a further move so one evening I put my arm round her. She didn't push me away or say, "Get off!" or "What are you up to?" And then a little fondling and cuddling, very innocent. She seemed to like it.

I like women in glasses. I like taking them off, I like putting them on. It's part of the ritual, because it's difficult making love with glasses on. They look so helpless when they take the glasses off, they make you feel powerful, particularly Emily, bless her. You'd take her glasses off and you could tell that she couldn't really see to walk about the room. She would blink and look at you as though, Oh, is that what you look like?

I never said anything about our relationship and neither did she. Emily was one that had to follow the rules – she wouldn't have liked anyone at the college to know about us – so in college we just ignored each other more or less. Sometimes we would go and stay

Barbara and the record player, Redcliffe Gardens.

•

with her father down in Patcham. I liked him, and he liked me and when we'd had our meal together he'd disappear up to his room so Emily and I would have the evening to ourselves.

Then I began my first teaching job so I didn't see so much of her then. But each time we saw each other we picked up where we'd left off. By this time I knew I loved her and she loved me. After a while I thought, next time she comes I'm going to try a bit of something else, I'm going to catch her with some music. I knew she loved classical music. At that time, in the early fifties, long-playing records were just being introduced. You could buy a boxed set, designed to play on the new type of record player. You could put the whole set on at once and they'd play automatically, one after the other. You hadn't to keep jumping up to change the record. You could play a whole opera right the way through if you wanted. I bought a set of Brahms sonatas. I lit candles and made the flat cosy and seductive – and took my chance. Brahms did the trick! After that we were really very intimate.

What lovemaking she had done before I do not know – you usually have some idea. She never mentioned any other girlfriends, never any indication she was making love with anyone else. Even if she was, I don't think she'd done much, because she was that bit older than me and very discreet – word didn't get round, what you can do and all the ways you can do it.

She was a bit like a lanky boy, had hardly any breasts at all, which was unusual for me. She'd got long, long legs, thin, and a long, thin body. She didn't have a beautiful face but it was a face that was alive – it was a face that was full of character. Sometimes you don't notice whether people have got high cheekbones or beautiful lips or a generous mouth, just catch the whole thing as ooh, she's got something. And she had, she'd got something.

By the time I realised I had to leave approved school work, Emily's father had died and she had the family house in Patcham to herself. She suggested I go and share the home.

"Try for a job in this district. If you wish to come and live with me, we could," – I always remember this speech – "we could live quite independently. The house is big enough and I'd be happy to have you there – a bit greedy having the house to myself." I got a job nearby, in Lewes, teaching in an ordinary girls' school.

Emily was a very, very good friend to me and I just adored her because she was so wise. I think I saw my mother in her. She took the place of my mother so I was lucky – a mother and a lover in one. It wasn't a fiery kind of love, it was mature, sincere, quite different from all the others. She was highly intelligent. She tried to educate me a bit, I think, and lift me up from the mundane sexual feelings that I felt.

We were discreet. She wouldn't have wanted the authorities to put a big 'L' in front of her name. We lived a serene life in the suburbs which was perfect for me at that time. I felt I'd been tossed about by the approved school work and Emily was very solicitous for my wellbeing and that I should quickly recover. She used to play the piano, beautifully and she taught me about gardening. I suppose people thought we were rather dull – we never went to the cinema, we never went dancing, we never went to a pub or a club. But we used to go to Glyndebourne. Every Christmas we'd choose which concerts we would go to that year. We made up a foursome with a couple of other women and had some very lovely times.

I'm sure the neighbours didn't suspect we were lesbians. Even Emily's friends didn't know about us. We kept separate bedrooms and we were careful not to show affection when they were around. Sometimes a 'sweetheart' or a 'darling' would slip out by mistake but I don't think they thought much of it. Lesbians were never mentioned – there was no such thing in those circles – you didn't say anyone was a lesbian. Emily and I didn't even mention it to each other. It all just happened.

I didn't know if Emily's close friend, Meg, knew we were making love. I didn't know what to make of Meg herself because she was living with a butchy friend for a long, long time. Basically I thought, Emily belongs to Meg – she's Meg's girl – they've known for years that they're going to live together so they must really love each other.

When Meg came to visit I would make myself scarce. I would go up to my flat in Redcliffe Gardens. On one occasion I went up with a friend I'd made at the school where I was teaching. I know her to this day. She knew I was a lesbian and she said, "Oh, I've never been made love to by a woman." So I said, "Well you want to try it. Come and stay the weekend at my flat. I'll show you what it's all about." She'd brought a lovely sexy nightie and we got into bed. We'd got nice music on, candlelight and everything seductive, but it was a complete fiasco. We finished up laughing. She just couldn't take it and I thought it was rather a lark too. We thought we'd better call that a day and cut out sex because she was really a man's woman.

I've never competed with men, I don't believe in competing with men. If a woman wants a man then leave them, clear off. Not that I don't think I could make a woman as happy as any man could. But if she wants to choose a man then go with a man – don't have me as well.

About twenty years ago it was fashionable to be a lesbian. I've got a bee in my bonnet about it. It was just the thing to be. A young woman perhaps with a baby, left her husband or he's left her and she looks around, finds a woman that she quite likes and says, "Oh, I'm a lesbian! Are you a lesbian? We're lesbian! Jump in the air!" But I think you're born a lesbian. Maybe something influences you to become an open lesbian. Maybe you're a latent lesbian all your life because you don't know how to express yourself and it never comes out. My queer friend, Cyril, used to talk about sleeping lesbians – that meant they were just sleeping together and not having sex. You still meet them today, those sort of people. You'd think by now they'd recognise what they are and go for it. But I don't think you can say, "Oh, I'm a happily married woman with two children and I like my husband's sister, I'm going to have an affair with her." Anyway if you're a lesbian you go for lesbians, you don't go for some attractive woman with a husband and children. You should never break into those relationships.

It was good having my London flat to escape to. But after several years I had a communication from the secretary of the Women's Pioneer Housing Scheme, saying if I wasn't going to live in it would I please relinquish it because other women were waiting. I remember to this day when I had posted the letter giving it up, it was on a Friday. I went to my bedroom and that night I just yelled my eyes out. I looked out of the window and I could just see the sea between the houses. I felt, what have I done? I've committed myself to this house with this woman. All right, I love her and she's a splendid woman but I've given up my flat. I always wanted a flat. I said, "You'll regret it."

Bless her heart, Emily never, never tried to claim me or possess me or make me feel I was tied to her, never – it was purely my own imagination, but I felt I must have my freedom.

I'd lived with Emily and worked in Lewes for four years. The head of the school was a sweetie and the other domestic science teacher, she was good, the girls were lovely, the staff were lovely but it was just so boring! Nice little girls coming for nice little cookery lessons with nice little baskets with nice little covers on. I thought, I'll never stick this. And Patcham was so boring! It wasn't even Brighton – if you went to the sea it was a day's trip from where we lived. Suddenly life in the suburbs seemed rather tame. I was always aware that I was only living with Emily until Meg retired and then I was supposed to push off. I decided to push off before I was pushed.

Emily was one of the most wonderful people I have ever met, so unselfish. I told her that I would like to go abroad. She said, "Well, look, you're forty-four, if you want to go abroad, you'd better be getting on with it because they won't want you, you'll be too old." So out came the educational supplement again and we were reading the places I could go. From all these lovely sounding places I decided I would go to Northern Nigeria. The country was to become independent in 1961 and they wanted Europeans to go out and train teachers. The Nigerians wanted their children to be educated. I was interviewed at Nigeria House by three Nigerians in their native costume, which pleased me because I thought, ah, at last I'm going somewhere really foreign. I was accepted.

It all seemed to happen quite quickly after that but I did fit in a visit to Italy before I went. You'd think I was going to the other side of the world! Particularly my 'mother', Mami, who thought she might never see me again. Mami took me to the church for the priest to bless me before I went off to Africa and she put her St Christopher round my neck. I've still got it to protect me on my journeys.

By the time I left for Nigeria, my sister, Midge, had got married. We used to ring each other every week and one Saturday she said, "I've just been married in Chelsea Registry Office." She could have knocked me down with a feather. I wasn't invited – I didn't even know she was contemplating marriage. I knew she wanted to have children. She said one of the reasons she loved her husband was because he showed her she was a woman. I think she was trying to prove to herself that she didn't need me any more. She was pregnant when I went to Nigeria.

17

Deep Blue with Yellow Splodges

You couldn't arrive in Africa and not have a soul to meet you. I was met from the boat at Lagos by someone from a women's colonial association, which supported women going to work overseas. She took me to the railway station to get the train to Kaduna. The railway stopped at Kaduna and the headmistress of the school I was going to drove me the remaining two hundred miles along a dirt track road. We were heading for Bornu Province, real Muslim country, and Maiduguri was the main town. It was just like I thought it might be: a mosque, little mud houses inside a walled compound, a few warehouse shops that looked like aircraft hangars and plenty of children and animals running about. There was a big market. It was a typical African market – you could change your money, you could buy any kind of foods. People used to come from the hills around carrying little bits of food on their heads that they'd grown themselves – mangoes, limes, all sorts of peppers. You never saw these in England then. It was a great big wonderland to me.

The Europeans' houses were all much the same verandah type – bungalows, quite big and they were all on the Government Residential Area. They were quite a distance from each other because there was a lot of space. So the next bungalow to me would be about a quarter of a mile. I had a whistle I blew if I wanted my neighbour's attention and she would come and blow the whistle back and then my boy would run with a message. I made good friends there, very constant friends.

I was, as usual, a bit of a rebel. All the ex-pats had cars. You had to have a car but I didn't – much to my boy's disgrace. The other boys would ask, "Why has your madam not got a car? Why does

Barbara at the market, Maiduguri, 1960.

•

she go about on a bicycle?" He was a bit ashamed about that. The ex-pats said, "How are you going to get to parties and things?" I said, "If people want me to join their social life they'll come for me and bring me back." They all belonged to the club and they all played tennis and they all went swimming at the club. I took one look at the club and I thought, well, that's not for me. I didn't want to waste my time sitting in a club with a load of Europeans, yapping and wife-swapping. A lot of the women liked to drink because they only had the club — you drank or you had a swim and then you drank again.

I took one look in the church and some sweet Nigerian girls were doing polishing and arranging flowers just before the service. They said, "We are allowed to stay for the service because we've cleaned the church. Only a few of us are allowed to come because it's the English service." I thought, oh hell to that, I'm not going in that church. So I joined in with the Catholic church and the old Irish fathers and the rough and tumble of it all – it wasn't so hypocritical.

Before I'd left England this women's colonial association had sent me lots of booklets of what to look out for, what to take and what to do. You'd to take salt pills to stop you dehydrating and look out for snakes. There were hardly any poisonous snakes but it described all about them and other nature things. In fact there was very little nature because of the heat. It was very hot always because the wind came direct from the Sahara. It was all sand but there are things will grow in sand – peanuts and zinnia flowers will grow in sand and neem trees which had long thin leaves and always seemed to be green. They attracted the water, they were the only trees we had. We always had a good water supply. The great big pipe ran along the main street which was mud and very occasionally it would split so your water was off for a while till it was mended. Peanuts were the main industry, if you could call it an industry. There were no factories, no margarine, they didn't make anything. They just sold peanuts, you'd see a great pyramid and it was all sacks of peanuts.

We'd been advised that we wouldn't be able to get sanitary towels in Nigeria and that we should use them to pack round our china instead of newspapers. You had to take all your own things out to set up a home, all packed in crates. So I took enough sanitary towels to last about a year or so, but I'd only been there a few weeks when the damn periods stopped and that was the end of it. I never saw it no more, so I was able to make presents of the things, and I still had some to use for packing when I came home.

I had several servants. You were given a whole book of printed notes about how to behave and how to treat your boys. It was strange because we'd never had servants in our family. James was my personal boy, he came to me by accident because Sambo, my real cook, kept disappearing off. One day James appeared, serving my dinner.

"Who are you?" I said.

"I'm James, madam. I'm your new boy."

I said, "What d'you mean? What about Sambo?" He said, "If you like me, I'm your new boy. I will tell you about Sambo when you've had your meal." So after I'd had the meal he took me to the door and showed me Sambo, propped up against a neem tree. I said, "Well, is he ill?" No, he'd been in jail for being drunk and, rather than me be with nobody, James had come to help me out. I said, "All right, if you do as I tell you and you're a good houseboy, I'll keep you." So I didn't choose him, he chose me. He was a very tall, handsome young man. No idea how old he was or when he was born and so he had to have my birthday so we could always remember it for official purposes. We decided he was about fifteen – so many rainy seasons, he must be fifteen.

The houseboys had their little brick-built hut just outside your back door, with a cooking part and a living part. You'd no cooking or smells going on in your house, it was all done in their quarters. Then we had a garden boy. I don't know what he did, swept the bits off the sand, I suppose, and perhaps watered your zinnias. And then there was a night watchman for the Government Residential Area. He was old as the hills. He wore a great, khaki, double-breasted army coat because it was cold often at night and he'd to sleep out on your verandah. Sometimes one of the servants would say, "Can you give me a little more money because I want to take a wife and she will help." So the wives used to come and go.

I loved it in school. We had perhaps a hundred and twenty girls. The classrooms were all round a big sandy compound and they lived in another compound, with little bedrooms where they slept. The

James, 1960.

•

gates were locked because they were Muslim girls. We had four Protestant girls, the others were Muslims. The only men were the old gardeners who were too decrepit to notice anything. The matrons were from the palace, the Shaihu's old concubines that he'd finished with. Big, fat, lovely women. We had a few Nigerian teachers for the crafts and we had a Nigerian scribe in the office, otherwise the staff were all white.

I went out as a domestic science teacher but I didn't know a damn thing. I didn't know how to make an oven out of an old ant hill or how to clap clay together to make a cooking pot. I knew what you did with a tomato or an egg but I didn't know what you did with cassava or sweet potato. They knew, they taught me. And we were supposed to teach such ridiculous recipes. They didn't want to know how to make a bloody rice pudding! When my time there ended, every girl wrote out a recipe for me. They nearly always had groundnuts in – groundnut stew, groundnut cakes, groundnut everything.

Their clothes were beautiful. Their traditional dress was called a zani. It just wrapped round their waist and tucked in, long. Because I was Domestic Science, I was in charge of dressmaking and sewing. The headmistress told me I had to get uniforms for the girls. I bought tie and dye material from the markets. Orange with black blobs – they were our school colours, black and orange. The seniors had deep blue with yellow splodges on. They sewed it up into these zanis. The girls had fabulous hairstyles, centre partings and a big plait that came down to a point on their foreheads. It looked so lovely, all of them standing there in a line, doing their cooking in their English-style white aprons. The ovens were concrete. Underneath was a wood fire and in the top were holes for putting the pans or bowls in.

They were training to go back to their villages to teach. If we had a very bright girl, she'd be watched and the headmistress would say, "She's a prospective one to send to England." The parents had to be approached and were very proud that their daughters were going to England to be trained to be a big teacher. We would get them ready to go into a different culture so that they didn't go in completely baffled. They went to Benenden, a real swanky girls' school in Kent. When they came back they belonged to the state and they could post them where they wanted.

We used to go round in a big wagon to the villages to interview children for new intake. On one of these trips James came with me. All through the journey back he said, "Oh, Madam, I wish I could be a pupil, I've always wanted to be a nurse..." So I went off to see the Irish fathers and I said, "Look, I've got this boy, he's fifteen and he wants to go to school, he's never been to school in his life, what can you do about it?" They said, "He'll have to bring his own chair because he can't sit at these little desks, he'll have to sit at the back in Class One with all the little ones, seven and eight." I said, "Oh fine, he'll do that. He'll come." So there was this great, tall boy with his inkpot and his pen stuck in his bushy hair, carrying his little case of books, so proud, walking off to school every day after that. And he did very well.

It was decided that, if he wanted to be a nurse, he would have to have a better standard of English than he would ever learn there, so he'd better come to England with me when I finally went home. I taught him a few little etiquettes and manners. I said, "Now you will use a lavatory like I have so you'd better rehearse. If you want to do big things, you go in and you sit down and then you pull the chain." One day he shouted, "Madam, come and look at me, I've done it." I went in and he was sitting on the lavatory with his back to me. He had to learn a few things that we just took for granted.

18

Two Crazy Ones

The biggest thing whilst I was in Nigeria was that I met Sheila, my last great love. I'd had my eye on her for a very long time. I first met her at the school. She was a nurse and she came round to give the girls medication. She also taught them how to mix medicines and diagnose simple things because they were going back to their villages and they would be in charge of little clinics that she would help set up. She always wore a spotlessly white uniform and she was obviously good at her job, which I admired. She had a little finger ring so I thought, she's got the ring. She always had her hair short and she walked with a bit of a stride which rather gave her away. She was a bit shorter than me, slim but not skinny, beautiful brown eyes. She had a good jaw and a lovely smile. I thought, yeah, I like her, she looks a bit of a lesbian, I'm going to make a beeline for her.

There was a homosexual in the education department, Bill. Everybody liked Bill and he was always giving mad parties. She was at one of his parties and we got in a corner of some room and started kissing. She said, "I knew, I knew, I knew, I knew!" I said, "You knew what?" She said, "I knew you were a lesbian, I knew you were attracted to me." I said, "Well, what are we going to do about it then?" She said, "Let's go home now." She made some excuse and off we went. What a night! No inhibitions – thirteen or fourteen times in one night – and then just once more!

After that she was nearly always in my house and James used to say, "That madam's been here again." He hated her. And he used to insult her by serving her with the wrong hand when he was serving food. It was the biggest thing that he could do – the hand he wiped his bottom with. He was so jealous of her.

Sheila.

•

"Is that madam coming again?"

I said, "That madam is Nurse Baker." He'd never heard of lesbians but he knew we liked sleeping together. He knew she used to run out of the house when he was coming on duty to make my breakfast because she'd got to be home for her breakfast and get ready for work. I'd push her out of bed and she'd run out barefoot, jump in the car and screech off in a cloud of sand. No chance of being discreet. Eventually she won him round.

It was a hot climate and it was a hot time. We got permission to go and swim in the irrigation tank in the agricultural area where they were growing lemons and oranges and mangoes. Beautiful cold water gushing into a deep tank – it was heavenly. We were always together. If one went to a party the other one went. We danced the way the local Nigerians danced. It was like disco dancing today but more subtle. It was very seductive – wooing, almost. You would stand on the spot and waggle your bum or waggle your breasts or move your arms gently. We found each other irresistible and we'd often go home early from some party we didn't like so we could jump into bed together.

It all added to the excitement, this illicit sleeping together because I don't think a lot of the women knew. There were quite a few professional women who were a bit secretive and you guessed something might be going on. But never out with it, saying, "I'm a lesbian, are you? Come to a lesbian party." The word was never mentioned. I think most of the men knew – the Fathers knew, certainly. They didn't care a damn if you gave them some money for the collection or a bottle of whiskey now and again. And the Italian men of course, they knew – they were a bit more intelligent about these things. No-one was bothered, they just thought we were those two crazy ones. It was very exciting, in a way, to be a lesbian because you were something unique. You were not run-of-the-mill.

I think with Sheila, she was the more dominant one and I was the weaker sex. She wanted to be in command and I went all simpery, feminine and wilty. I wanted to go into character so I would dress to feel the part. Usually a butchy woman would want her partner to look like she belonged to her and so you would do it to please her, besides pleasing yourself. And she'd say if she didn't like something: "I think you look awful in that dress, for heaven's sake take it off." Or you'd buy something new, she'd say, "Oh you look beautiful in it, yes, wear it."

Sheila had a big, black Ford Ensign, which could hold all her medical equipment and her retinue of boys when she was going into the bush. We went in it on a trip to Chad, French West Africa. We'd met a homosexual Frenchman who'd invited us to visit him there. Going along the road to Chad it was like going through the desert. You sometimes couldn't see where the road was. It was all sand – not soft sand like you see in films but hard, in deep ripples and ruts. The heat was killing.

Barbara outside her bungalow on the Government Residential Area.

•

I was wearing a blue dress – it was like a gymslip, square neckline but it had little concertina pleats all the way round, top and bottom – a flowing thing. It had a tie belt round the middle and when you put that round it showed your figure off. It was just like a tent, really. It was one of Sheila's favourites. She used to get really worked up when I wore it. It was so voluminous I could put it over her legs and my legs. Her hand could easily roam anywhere – took the belt off and it could roam anywhere more still. It used to thrill me no end. I took it for granted that she could do anything. Why shouldn't she drive this heavy car with one hand, manoeuvre over the ruts and make love to me at the same time? It was very dangerous and I knew it was, which made it more exciting. When we crossed the border into French territory there was a tarmac road and she could speed along. It wasn't so exciting then. We were always making love while she was driving. I did admire her with that car.

When Sheila went into the bush on Sunday mornings to give medicines or inoculations she'd say, "Are you coming with me?" So I used to get to all these strange places that other people didn't get to. That was the first time I ever saw a baby being born. Somebody had run in the early evening, come with a lantern, saying, "Please come, Madam, my wife is with child. It's the first child and we want you to help." It was in a grass hut, all dark. A woman was holding up a little oil lantern while the mother was giving birth. There's this lovely pink cavern and out comes a little curly piece of black stuff. I thought, whatever's that? Forgot she was a black woman at that moment – and of course, it was the baby's head.

Sheila was always getting babies given her. A fella would come and say, "We want you to have our baby." They thought it was terrible that this lovely lady didn't have any children of her own. They would bring a newborn baby as a gift. And she'd say, "Well, thankyou very much." She'd keep it for two days and then she'd take it back and say it was crying for its mother. Always having babies given her. It was a nice idea – if a woman didn't have any children, say she wasn't married, a sister or a relative would give her a baby and it was hers to keep – none of this fancy adoption business. You had to have a baby. No-one gave me any, thank God.

Sheila loved babies, loved children. She said to me once, "If I could conceive, become pregnant, have a baby, would you accept it?" I said, "No. Are you dead serious?" She said, "Yes. I would like us to have a baby and bring it up as ours." That was way out, talking like that in the sixties. I mean, now they're talking about it, openly and freely but it was a wild idea in those days. She was serious but I didn't want a kid coming, interrupting our life. No. I don't particularly like babies, anyway. If I could have given her a baby, it would have been a different thing, if it had been our baby. But I couldn't bear the thought of some man having intercourse with her to give her a baby – it was just, to me, a horror story. I still think if you're a lesbian, you'd never want a man. I've never had a man in my life and I've never wanted one. And to think that she wanted a man inside her just horrified me. I said, "If you want a baby, you'll have to go with a fella and marry him and live with him. Don't come back to me if a fella's been poking you around." There was no talk of artificial insemination then. So that was that – a few tears and it soon fizzled out.

My tour finished before Sheila's so I came back to England before her but we had decided that we would set up home together. James came back with me. We stopped off at the Holy Land because he was a very religious boy and wanted to see all the things he'd read about in the Bible. He particularly wanted to see snow, which was ironic really because when we stepped out of Brighton station we were knee-deep in the bloody stuff. It was January '63, there'd been a blizzard and no taxis or buses could get through so we had to walk all the way to Patcham. The snow was deep and it took hours. I told James to tread in my footprints, like Good King Wenceslas.

I was staying with Emily who had been very understanding about me and Sheila and given us her blessing. James stayed nearby. Mrs Crabtree, a good friend I'd made when I was teaching in Lewes, paid for his tuition at the Davis school. He had a happy time. He loved my sister, Midge and her two young boys. When they came down to Brighton we'd all spend the day on the beach together. He did very well at school and got his certificate. After a year, he went back home and passed his first nursing exam. But he couldn't get beyond that so after some time he gave up nursing and eventually went back to his village. He writes to me now and says, "Madam, you must be very old, you must come to Nigeria and I can look after you and nurse you till you die." So I've got a home to go to if I want to go to a village in Nigeria.

I could have been easily persuaded to stay in Nigeria. When you've once been to Africa there's always something of you left behind there, always. So when you come back and see a black face your heart opens up and you smile and you want to be friends with them. There's a woman who lives round the corner from me now. I met her in the fishmonger and she was buying a bit of this and a bit of that. I said, "I can guess what you're going to make, fish soup." I was speaking slowly because I thought she couldn't under-stand me but she spoke in perfect English back to me. I asked her to show me how to make fish soup and now we're real friends. She says it takes five years for her to make a friend. She puts them to the test and if they're still friends after five years they're friends for life. And that's what's happened. We are friends for life now.

19

Just for a While You Could Be Free

While Sheila was finishing her tour in Nigeria, I was commissioned to find somewhere for us to live. We wanted a little house and we wanted it to be in Brighton – not for the club life, never went to any clubs although there were plenty of queer clubs around. I liked the interesting little streets and the beach. I'd known the town for a long time, since the war when a group of us from the police had come down a couple of times in a car, just for a day out. The seafront was covered in barbed wire then, against enemy invasion. And then Tonks and I used to come here when we were doing our teacher training. We'd walk along the cliff top and then go back home, just to get some fresh air.

I loved going to Black Rock and underneath the rock, splashing and climbing over the boulders in the sea, turning over stones to find crabs. It was heavenly. They've done away with all that now.

I was staying up in Patcham with Emily and I thought, what's the point of living in a seaside place if it's a day's march to the sea? If Sheila and I are going to have a house here it's got to be near the sea.

I would start out in the early morning, after Emily had gone to work, with a map of Brighton drawn out in squares. Each day I went methodically up and down all the streets in one square. I can't tell you how many houses I looked at and went into and wrote about to Sheila, saying, "Shall we have this?" And she always sent the same reply, "I'll leave it to you. If you like it, I'll like it." The weather was bitter and I used to almost be crying with cold when I went back in the afternoon to Emily. Finally I went down a quiet little cul-de-sac, not far from the Peace Statue on the seafront.

There, the last house at the bottom had a big paper in the window saying 'Keys with George White, Estate Agents'. I thought, cute little street, lovely window boxes next door. Ooh, this looks like the place, I'm sure this is it.

We got it at auction for three thousand pounds. Sheila and I put in a thousand pounds each and we borrowed a thousand from Brighton Borough Council, which you could do then. I busied myself making a home for the two of us. I got a job teaching handicapped children, which I loved because it was a challenge and I felt I was doing something worthwhile. So I was very happily in this house and in a job when Sheila's tour ended and she came home.

We had a blissful year together. Sheila really spoiled me – it almost got to the point where I didn't dare say I liked something because she'd buy it for me, there and then. She really loved me and wanted to give me things. She gives the impression she might be a little bit hard and she isn't, she's as soft as my pocket.

I always liked the bedroom to be the most decorative room. In our little house I wanted the bedroom ceiling gold. Sheila bought half a gallon of gold paint. It's all runny, gold paint, very difficult to use. God knows how she did it but it looked marvellous when it was done. She used to love doing all those kinds of things. I have a piece of furniture now in my bedroom that somebody was throwing out. Sheila stripped it all down by hand and french-polished it – all properly with linseed oil and the little pad.

Once we were settled, I got involved in the Minorities Research Group, of all names, which was a sort of lesbian club based in London. If I remember rightly, it was begun by two persons, Esmé Langley and Diana Chapman. Diana Chapman had written a lesbian article in some magazine which was seen by Esmé Langley. She liked this article and thought she would like the person so she got in touch and thereby started a correspondence. This was 1963 sometime and they soon got together and formed the MRG. They met monthly just behind Liberty's off Regent Street at the Shakespeare's

Head. I heard of it through the *Sunday Telegraph*, I believe. It was one of those little tiny adverts. There weren't any gay magazines that I knew of, like they've got now, *Pink Paper* and God knows what – everything was hush-hush. They were quite literary people, they really knew what they were doing and they started *Arena Three*, the first lesbian magazine in this country.

I wrote and they said come up for a meeting. I just barged into this place one evening and introduced myself. And God, it was a crowd! We used to sit at tables and converse and perhaps have some refreshments and circulate round and Esmé Langley might give a little talk. I was very impressed and when they asked for a representative for the South Coast, I stood up and volunteered for the work.

My job was to support lesbians who were having trouble with their relationships or make contact with those who felt isolated. The organisers would write to me from London or phone me if somebody wanted help or wanted to come and see me. Finding out about this club seemed like a salvation to these women – before then they were floundering around not knowing, just as I didn't know years before in Blackburn.

Often they wanted us to go to see them. Sheila bought a fast car. It was a Bond Equipe, which sounds like a three-wheeler but it wasn't – it was a racing-type car, dark green, a smart little number. We zoomed along the coast and round the countryside right from Chichester almost to Hastings visiting these lesbians who were heartbroken or who were having rows, and really counselling them. It was nearly always one of them been deserted by the other, that was the common story, how should she cope with it? Sheila would drive off somewhere or sit in the garden whilst I was seeing how I could help. Usually they were very pleased to hear from you – you were a lifeline – but one couple were very snobby. When I rang, a posh voice said, "I don't think we really need a visit from you – we don't want the neighbours to see you coming to the door." I said,

"Well, I'm not a screaming lesbian and I haven't got wings or horns." But she said, "I think we're managing, thank you very much." I suppose they were scared.

Sometimes they just wanted to know where they could meet other lesbians so I had the double role of helping them where I could but also of playing hostess, inviting them to my house and introducing them to each other. We got a nice little social group going in the end. We would do the rounds of each other's homes, rarely more than eight or nine of us but it was a wonderful thing because you could just let your hair down and be natural. It made a big difference to Sheila and me coming back from the social life and the luxury we'd had in Nigeria. It would all have been a bit mundane without it.

A very young nurse rang me – they all had my number. She was in love with a sister who'd left her to go off with another sister so this kid was absolutely bereft. She was going berserk. She really just needed a mother figure – someone to comfort her and listen – but I always felt I had to be careful because her antennae were out, looking for somebody. I felt if I gave her the slightest encouragement I'd be entangled and that's one thing I had to be careful about as a rep. We were told, never, never, never – if by some fluke you fancied somebody – you just laid off. She did everything to find a partner – even advertised in *Arena Three* – but she just could not find the right person. She would have made a wonderful partner for somebody but she seemed to attract the wrong ones. Some people do, I think.

There was one old lady – my lovely Miss Ellis. I shouldn't call her an old lady because she was only seventy-four and I'm eighty-four and don't call myself an old lady. She was passed on to me as somebody who needed help. She'd been married to a Dutch woman – I think it was fifty-odd years they'd been together. What an example! They'd lived at Peacehaven and when her partner'd died she was utterly and absolutely heartbroken. I thought I'd never do anything with her. I just used to go and listen to her stories about her friend and their life together. Sometimes she'd come to my house, stay the night and I'd give her all the best things in the bedroom or give her a bath to make her feel nice. There was never anything between us, she just liked some loving care, a bit of consideration. We became very good friends. She used to make donations to MRG which we'd never had before, substantial sums of money because although she wasn't rich, she'd nobody to look after then – she had relatives but they weren't close to her.

I remember there was a funny one – I call her a funny one, not with disrespect, she just really made me laugh to look at her. She was very short and stocky and butch and it screamed from her: "I am a lesbian." She was a social worker, a big-hearted girl, soft as a puppy. She bought two seventeenth-century cottages next to each other so she could make a big place. We all mucked in to help get it prepared for the builders. She found all kinds of hidden treasures under the walls, little paintings and trap doors.

Whilst this disturbance was going on she preferred to live in a caravan in the garden. So when it was her turn to have us to visit, we all squashed into this caravan and behaved like a lot of kids. It was lovely just to let off steam. You couldn't dance, it was too tiny but we used to tell what we thought were dirty jokes or risqué jokes and tell of our experiences. We were able to discuss our lives quite openly – I suppose it was like being in the psychiatrist's chair really, so good for us all.

We were trying to find somebody for this social worker and after a while she met a very feminine woman, very middle-class who told us her father was Anthony Chenevix-Trench, headmaster of Eton. She showed us a photograph of her in her Wrens outfit looking very attractive and we all thought she was lovely. Then we got a terrible shock – it was front page news in one of the Sunday papers that this woman was running a nursing home and she'd had some of the inmates make wills in her favour. She'd been inheriting lots of

5, Norfolk Buildings today.

●

money and living in grand style. She was exposed as a fraud and sent to prison and it turned out she was no relation whatsoever to this well-known family! So then of course the poor partner was heart-broken because she'd fallen completely in love with her, so we'd to nurse her along. We never found anybody else for her.

Our house seemed to be the base. It felt very daring to have meetings in your home, although we were lucky – we were at the end of the cul-de-sac so there were only a few curtains that could be drawn aside and peeped out of. We were tucked away in a little secret street. We used to periodically put on these do's. We'd dance our heads off – I suppose you'd call it having a disco nowadays. Our next-door neighbour didn't care what we did. We'd say, "Oh, we're having a party tonight... we might be making a bit of noise but if you can't beat us join us."

If you're behaving yourself and you look happy, I think the

neighbours respect you. They don't think, oh, that awful gang's meeting again. You've got to get a good name. Why shouldn't we have a good name? We're good people. Sometimes in the street people would call after Sheila and me, particularly young people, call abuse at us and snigger.

"Couple of lezzies! What do you do in bed then? What's wrong with men?"

We just walked on, used to giggle and walk on. We didn't mind. We didn't care.

I remember once our little group met on the beach at Worthing. We all had to bring something towards the tea, it was mackerel or something quite humble and we cooked them on an open fire – collected bits of wood and made a fire like a lot of little Girl Guides. All these stupid people were looking at this gang of women making fires on the beach. I suppose they thought we were quite cranky. But we enjoyed it.

MRG didn't last very long – I think it was about three years. Then it fell apart because there was jealousy and competition in the hierarchy. There was a splinter group which broke away because they didn't agree with the organisers. The Kensington and Richmond branch wrote to everybody, do you want to join our group? They became known as Kenric which is still going today. We carried on locally for a while but without the support from London we soon fizzled out which was sad. It had been wonderful to go to these things where you could just be yourself, no need to pretend, no need to be afraid of making a glance or a gesture or say what you thought. Just for a while you could be free. I think MRG did a damned good job.

20

You Can't Live on Condiments

After a time my relationship with Sheila began to get a bit dicey. Our feet had never really been on the ground in Nigeria and when we came back to England it was a different kind of living from what we'd had. We hadn't the servants, we hadn't the sunshine, we hadn't the money. We had to face the facts of living and the hardships of living. Sheila was very dissatisfied with her work because in Nigeria she'd been kingpin and done everything. Coming back and getting a mundane job nursing, going round schools TB testing and all that boring stuff, it must have been purgatory for her. She was a mere nobody.

Sheila always did like to drink and I didn't. She wanted to watch television and I didn't. So there were rows. I kept silent because it takes two to make a row and I'm not a rowy person. She could shout and row her head off and I'd just sit there, quietly or move out the way somewhere, which probably made her more angry. She would get very aggressive and even throw things around the place, throw the glass on the wall with all the wine in. She never hit me but she had a very abusive tongue. We were both terribly hurt and I think we both knew we were hurting each other but we couldn't stop it. Emily tried to help. She knew how much I loved Sheila and she'd try to placate us if we were rowing or help us see where we were going wrong.

Then Sheila started to go and visit her friend, Pam, who'd just split up from her partner – "She'll have a bottle of wine with me." So there were the two of them, one more or less abandoned and the other very dissatisfied with life and with me. They drew to each other and the drinking sessions started.

I was disillusioned with life, completely, that this could happen to the one person I'd finally wanted to be with – that she'd rather drink a bottle of wine with someone else than do something interesting with me. I would go to bed and just let her come home. I wouldn't even wait up for her. I was sewing for her – she wanted a lot of new white aprons and she didn't like any that she could buy. I'd be crying and so upset that she wasn't there with me and I used to let my tears drop all over the bloomin' machine and all over the material.

I took time off work. The doctor gave me pills which I was taking as a kind of sedation. I had been off for some time and Mrs Crabtree came to see me, sweet old thing. She said, "What is the doctor giving you? I think he's half doping you – your speech is a bit slurred, you're walking very slowly and you're not quite with it. I know you've had some trouble, what is it?" I told her and she said, "Well, I don't think you should go on taking these. Find out why you're like this and sort it out. You've got to start to want to live." And while she was there she made me chuck all the pills away down the lavatory.

Sheila and I were very much in love. But there's a limit to how many times you can make love. That's not living, making love, it's condiments to living. You can't live on condiments all the time. She loved the house, she loved me getting it all ready but there was, deep down, that little resentment that she hadn't built it with me. There was a suggestion one time that it wasn't her house.

Another problem was that Sheila was jealous of my sister and her children. Midge's marriage was breaking down and I wanted to feel that I was there for her if I was needed. If I was anxious about some crisis they were having I'd just bolt up to London to look after them. Midge loved her husband but he was coming and going all the time and telling lies. She couldn't take much more. She didn't want the children to see her weeping or not knowing what to do next. My sister was my priority – her and her children. I felt

Midge and the boys on the South Downs.

•

responsible for them and tried to fill the gap their father was leaving.

Sheila thought, why can't she leave them alone, why does she want to get involved – she's mine now. I've sometimes wondered, if I'd played my cards differently – I don't know how differently – would she have been different? It could have been a wonderful thing if Sheila had accepted Midge and her boys because they wanted to accept her. Looking back, I think maybe she should have had lots of children. It was something that was missing from her life. And I had that little niggle, thinking, I can't give her what she wants.

We thought we would destroy each other if we went on as we were so we ought to live apart for a while – one of us must go away. We decided to apply for jobs abroad again, since we both loved it abroad, and whoever was accepted first would go. I got an interview to go to Hong Kong – they wanted to start a school for educationally subnormal children but that project fell through. Sheila had a job offered in Kota Kinabalu, so off she went to Malaysia, both of us brokenhearted. But it had to be done.

I'm thankful now that I had a job to go to, although at the time I didn't realise it. I've noticed over the years that people who have troubles get over them a lot quicker if they've got to get up and go to work. It was necessary for my survival at that time that the type of work I was doing was the type of work where they needed me. I was needed and loved by loads of children. And respected by staff alike. You can't do that type of work, with handicapped children, and not give your full mind to it. You have to set aside the painful things that are going on.

I also found consolation with Emma, a friend I'd come to know through the Minorities Research Group. After one of the MRG meetings in London, when they were all milling about, saying farewells, a woman had come up to me. She was attractive-looking, bobbed hair, very vivacious. She said, "I live in Sussex, can I meet you because I'd like to have a talk? I'm having a bit of trouble with my friend." She and her friend lived in Wilmington and Sheila and

I went over quite a few times. I used to think it was heavenly going there. The village in the springtime was filled with snowdrops and they had a Romany caravan and a donkey. We would have little tea parties on the lawn.

They always made us welcome but Emma's partner, every time, was always trying to put her down. I think she was showing that she was boss, she was the butchy one. Emma felt a bit shut in and wanted more company. So things were getting difficult for her with her friend. My job as rep was to keep people together and encourage them to forgive and forget and start again. But when things got difficult for me with Sheila, I found myself turning to Emma. I was heartbroken, she was dissatisfied with her relationship. How often this happens – by comforting each other, eventually you fall in love!

Emma always seemed pleased to see me whatever I was doing. She'd come with her little Triumph Herald car and shout up at the window and I'd be eager to run down and get in. You could jump in without opening the door. I felt quite exhilarated – thought I was a sports girl – sitting in this little red car with the hood down, swishing through the countryside. She always did things with a bit of style. She was a painter. We heightened each other's feelings and vision. We saw things you might not usually notice – a line of trees or the shape of a hill. Sheila was more silent about things and even gave the impression she might be bored sometimes.

The chemistry was there between Emma and me. I wasn't being satisfied sexually because although Sheila and I were making love it wasn't true to me – it was like a consolation prize – and certainly Emma wasn't getting any sex at all. I would go and visit her sometimes when her friend was at work – we'd fly into each other's arms like two magnets. Didn't matter where it was, frantically making love, on the floor, behind the door, in the caravan, anywhere. My God, we were like raving lunatics, you'd think we'd never had it before. It was wonderful. It makes me tickle to think of it. It was quite spontaneous, "Ooh! Ooh! We've got five minutes, we've got

Barbara, Syria, Emma, Gina at 5, Norfolk Buildings.

•

ten minutes. Quick! Quick!" In the car and all, in the middle of
Ashdown Forest. It wasn't all one person or the other; it was just
mutual. Boom! Bang!

On one occasion Emma and I had abandoned the car and taken
a walk on the Downs between Sussex University and Ditchling
Beacon. We couldn't hold it any longer, found some bushes, got
behind these bushes, frantically making love. You need the right
atmosphere for making love. Out in the open you've got a different kind of atmospherics around you. No music, only birdsong, a
skylark up in the air. And always the fear that somebody will come
past – that's very exciting.

When I got home I found I'd lost my St Christopher chain that Mami gave me. So I said, "I must find it, I must find it! It's on the Downs somewhere." She said, "Well, there's only one place where it could be, we'll go and look tomorrow." We went and looked under the one bush that we could hide behind, grovelled about and there it was. Incredible!

Later on we spent nights together when she was free and I was free. She asked me several times would I live with her. I think we would have got on all right but by then I was afraid to go into a permanent relationship because of Sheila, I was too heartbroken. Emma came to Brighton, lived round the corner from me and I know in her secret heart she was hoping that she would eventually win me over. She'd say, "Why not try it again because I'm not Sheila and I will be different? But anyway, was it not worth the suffering?" And I weighed it up: I thought, no, not really. I couldn't go through that again, not for anybody. She eventually gave up and moved to Kent. We still see each other. I wouldn't like to lose Emma, she does mean a lot to me. I love Emma. I'm not in love with her but I love her.

21

A Crusade for Women

Sheila had been in Malaysia about a year when I discovered I'd got breast cancer. I think it was when there was a scare and they were saying, "You must feel and see if you've got anything unusual." I felt a little lump and I thought, I'd better do something about this. So I went to my doctor who sent me to a specialist. They wanted me to go into hospital very quickly.

I had about three days. I went through everything. I was up practically all night going through drawers, paying any unpaid bills and writing any outstanding letters. I was sure I was going to die and I thought, if I don't come round, I don't want to leave evidence for anybody to scrummage around in. So I burnt anything that gave away my relationships with anyone else. Love letters from Sheila and Trudi, all tied up with ribbon, old-fashioned like you used to do, pictures of nude women, a lot of photos of Sheila and me taken in Nigeria, little bits of fancy underwear, and other belongings of that sort. I put everything in the dustbin, loosened them all up and put a match to them. I knew they wouldn't burn if I put the lid on so I stood and watched them. They were my secrets, they were my life, they belonged to me and the person they were related to – they weren't for anybody to see and open, laugh at or use. I was sorry afterwards because I didn't die after all. I'd also had a lot of pin-ups pasted inside my bathroom, nothing vulgar, just pictures of beautiful women that I'd got from magazines or from photographs, but I left those. I thought, it's just too bad if they don't like those.

God, I'm always looking at women! In the hospital I had a woman doctor and I fell for her a big load. She knew, she used to play up like mad – if she went to London for her day off, she'd bring me back a card from some museum she'd been to. She'd say, "I've brought this card back because I think she looks like you, she's got her hair done like you." Or she'd bring me a little basket for strawberries. Anyway, when it came to the operation, I said, "If I'm to have this operation, I want you to do it." She said, "Oh no, I can't do it, the consultant will do it." I said, "I'm not having it done, then. I'm not having a man's hands on me." When it came next morning she said, "It's all right, I'm going to do it." Oh thank God, I thought. She said, "When we have a look at you, if we can save it, we will. But it may mean that you have to have the breast removed, so I'm warning you."

Sheila sent me a ring with instructions to wear it during the operation, "It'll bring me close to you." When I wakened up I didn't know if the breast was on or off – didn't dare ask, didn't dare feel. It was off. I felt dreadful. I took it rather badly because I'm a titmouse – I think it's such a beautiful part of a woman. I think the breasts are the most beautiful part really – maybe it's because men don't have them. To think I only had one breast was just the end. I felt nobody would ever love me again. This must be the end of my sex life – how could they possibly want to make love to me in that state? It would have to be me making love to them all the time which might get a bit boring.

I went to Italy for my convalescence. When Mr Carbone met me at the airport he said, "Oh, you have not got the face of an operated woman!" That cheered me up. But it took a lot of getting over because I really felt mutilated. I wore big, floppy men's shirts after the operation, with the sleeves rolled up – things that didn't show my shape. When I was in shops, trying clothes on, I would make excuses: "You see, I'm deformed, that's why it doesn't hang properly." I despised myself.

After a while I was given a false bosom which was pretty awful, something like those stiff cups they used to put in swimsuits. One of my sister's boys, who was then about five, he thought it was a great joke. When he met me, he used to run and get hold of this artificial bosom and go, "Beep, beep! Beep, beep!" squeezing the thing. He helped me because he made fun of it and laughed about it.

The hospital gave me some awful band thing to put round. It was thick, white cotton, cumbersome and ugly. You'd to go to a corsetier they had on their books and they measured you – actually measured you and made it for you – but it was still cumbersome. I said, "I'm not wearing that." I was angry. Why should I go about with this awful bra? I felt I couldn't undress. The woman at the corsetiers said, "Well, we've nothing else, you'll have to. You have to have it very firm to hold it all in." I said, "But it's not going to fall out – that's my business if it falls out." I kept going and complaining and asked to see somebody in authority about these things. I felt I was on a bit of a crusade for women. I took a bra that I'd bought, a pretty, lacy thing.

"Why can't you issue something like this for us? Why do we have to have these foul things? Why don't you say we can go and buy our own?"

So I've got very pretty bras now – lace and decorations and bows. It helps make you feel better.

Then these new bosoms came in. I was thrilled with mine – when you touch it, it feels like one of your own bosoms. It's like stiff blancmange and it falls about in shape like your bosom does. It's got a little tiny blob so it shows through your blouse like a nipple. There's a wonderful woman at the corsetiers in charge of a lot of shoe boxes with names and measurements on them. She's been there for years, so lovely and sympathetic. She just puts your real bosom in her hand then she goes and looks at a number and pulls out a box and opens it and says, "I think that'll be your fit, dear, try that one."

The doctor and I kept in touch for a while – she used to come to my house, I used to look all goofy-eyed and take flowers to the hospital for her. I've got a thing about women doctors – they look such angels. And years after, I was sitting in the corridor, waiting for my check-up and along came this woman with papers under her arm, looking very businesslike. She gave me a glance and said, "I know you, you're Barbara Bell."

"Good Lord," I said, "You're the doctor."

We chatted a bit and she said she was head of this and doing the other. I said, "But look, you must have had dozens of women come through your hands, I'm flattered but how do you come to remember me?" She said, "Because you were the first operation I ever did and I was terrified. And I must apologise because when I came to the end, I'd got a bit too much, I had to put a tuck in." I said, "I never noticed." She said, "Well, I got hauled over the coals for it."

I was fifty-three when I had the operation. I've not had any new lovers since. There was a person I met who lived in the country. I knew she really liked me and I was physically attracted to her. As I was going over to see her, at the back of my mind all the time was, if we start making love, what is she going to say, what am I going to do? And when we were near to getting the last clothes off, I said, "You will have to understand, I don't think I can go on with it." I couldn't even tell her what it was, I was too sensitive about it.

I took it all very, very badly. People didn't know I did – even my sister didn't know I did – but I didn't dare look at myself. My old lovers were very understanding when we made love. They never saw my mastectomy scar. They knew I felt deformed so they never pressed me to look at it or feel it. It never dampened my ardour but I always had to be covered up. I wore a little black fancy vest during lovemaking. Sheila didn't care a damn about it and after a time I did come to forget at the proper moments.

22

A Dream That Didn't Come True

Sheila always came home to me when she had leave, usually about six weeks a year and often we would go on holidays together. On her first leave we went for a month to North Africa. She got a fast car, a Volkswagen Karman Ghia – she had it brought from Germany to the front door of our house. We went to the AA who in those days planned a route for you. We motored all the way down, through France, through Spain, went to Portugal because we wanted to see as much as we could on the way.

We stayed in Tangiers in a block of flats – now it's all built-up with flats but then it wasn't a tourist place at all. I fell in love with the native quarter, the old city of Tangiers within the city walls. Little narrow passages. Houses all clinging together with steps on the outside, whitewashed and clean. Lovely, smelly restaurants – it was very, very much native.

We went to visit an old lesbian who ran a bookshop. She bought books very cheaply from boys at the hotels who collected up after tourists. She was a very clever woman, perhaps mid-European. It was obviously a meeting place for local homosexuals. She would sit on a high stool behind a counter just inside the door so they all used to loll in the doorway. It was a wonderful place to meet and they made a fuss of us so we felt very welcome there. Every night the homosexuals paraded down one of the boulevards, walking hand in hand or sat at tables outside the Café de Paris, quite brazenly.

Things didn't go too well between Sheila and me. The AA, because we had this fast car and a good driver, they thought we wanted to cover a lot of miles. They planned a route including all the places we'd told them – Fez, Casablanca, Marrakech – which meant doing about 350 miles a day. Well, in a hot climate 350 miles is a lot to cope with. Sheila was tired all the time. We'd arrive at our hotel each day and she'd just want to flop on the bed while I was eager to explore. I didn't appreciate how hard it was. I'd only driven in Nigeria where there were long, straight, metal roads. You just pushed yourself in a ditch to let the mammy wagons pass or in the village you just went round a little pile of newly-born puppies or had an ostrich running alongside your car – nothing more dangerous than that.

On the mountain roads in North Africa, you'd think there wasn't a soul in sight. Then you'd go round a hairpin bend and there would be some little urchin Arab boy with a few leaves containing a bunch of grapes or holding out a semi-precious stone. I'd say, "Oh, stop, let's!" And she'd say, "Can't stop. Can't stop here. How do you think I can stop here?" I expected her to take it all in her stride.

We did stop at one village in the middle of the day because I wanted to find something for us to drink. We were only a little way off our destination so I said, "Why don't we have a picnic on the way? We could get some meat and cook it." Of course, everything was shut up – mad dogs and Englishmen out in the midday sun, that was us. So I left Sheila in the car and went swanning around trying to find a butcher who'd open his shop or some place where we could have a bottle of 7-Up. Meanwhile, a gang of urchins had scrambled in the back of the open car. They'd pinched Sheila's hat, pinched her camera, they were laughing and running off and she was furious. I came back, saying, "Look at this lovely meat," and she said, "You get in this car and I don't want to look at any bloody meat."

I was a trial. I didn't realise what a trial until a long time later on. How did she put up with me taking it all for granted? I thought she was just a chauffeur. I tried to make it up to her, though, because we really did love each other. Mostly it was a very physical

Sheila on the North Africa trip, 1966.

•

love but there was something else there as well, something very deep. It was too passionate, really – we shouldn't have had all that physical and then it would have been perfect. But you can't help it if that's where you're attracted to.

Although we found it difficult being together, when we were apart it was another story – desperately wanting each other again. We used to write loving letters – it's surprising what you can do in a letter. A friend of mine admitted to me the other day that she'd been phoning her lover and had really enjoyed it very much –

reached a climax talking to her over the phone. It used to happen to us just by letter. They were wonderful letters, very, very intimate.

In 1975 Sheila had the idea that on her way home from Borneo we should meet in Delhi and go for a holiday on a houseboat on Lake Kashmir. It was beginning to be a love-hate relationship between us – we couldn't do without each other yet we couldn't do with each other. I think she thought that we could recapture something, that we could reclaim some lost ground. She sent the money for the holiday direct to a travel agent in Norfolk Square in Brighton. The fella running it was a homosexual. He was a lovely fella, dead now and he was all for this holiday, telling all his friends I was going to meet my lover out there.

At the time I had a little pop-pop motorbike, a Triumph, and I didn't half fancy myself with it. I had a blue cotton trouser suit and a blue helmet. When I was on the road people used to turn round and wave – they thought I was an RAC man. I was going along New Church Road in Hove one day when a car came out of a turning on the opposite side of the road and just ploughed into me. I got a broken leg. So that was that, the holiday had to be scrapped. The travel agent was just as heartbroken as I was. I wired Sheila to say I couldn't come and she sent a telegram back: "No matter where we meet, love you." So that was a dream that didn't come true. I suppose I'd looked on it as a second honeymoon – might have been a very different life now had it all come off.

Sheila came home for her holiday and we spent a couple of weeks in the West Country. She was nearing the end of her tour in Borneo and the plan was that she would come and live with me again. When she went back I thought, I can't live like this, I've just got to be on my own. I couldn't bear all the ups and downs. I wrote and said, "Do you really want to come back here?" We decided that we would part for good.

Sheila was to have half of everything we'd put into the house – she could have her thousand pounds back and half of all the mort-

Miss Ellis.

•

gage payments. Miss Ellis, my dear friend from MRG, said, "How you going to do all this?" I said, "I don't know but I can't go on in this agony." One day, when she'd been for a meal and she'd gone off in the taxi, she left a carrier bag down at the side of the chair. It was tied up at the top so I thought, oh well, she'll be coming for it. Then she rang, "There's a carrier bag down at the side of the big chair." I said, "Yes, I've seen it." She said, "Well, it's for you, open it." It was a thousand pounds. A third of the cost of our house – in cash, in a carrier bag. Because she felt for me and the state I was in.

When Sheila came back to England she got a job with Hove district nurses. She lived in nurses' quarters and I used to go and visit her sometimes. I found it thrilling to go and see this person I'd loved all those years. I used to get collywobbles – dress myself up and paint my face and look as attractive as ever I could. We used to flirt like mad – even after all we'd been through. But there was never any question of us getting back together. She and Pam, her drinking pal of old, decided they would team up and buy a house in Hove. I had no desire to encroach on their relationship. I just loved to see Sheila and be in her company.

And when we're together now there's still a charge, like an electrical current passing from one to the other. But she can still come out with nasty hurtful things. She came to visit me recently and we were reminiscing about Nigeria. She'd had a few drinks and we were dancing by candlelight to an African record. We were really, really gone with this music and she kept shouting, "Ayae, ayae, ayae," like they used to and coming out with odd words of Hausa – she could speak quite a bit of their lingo. And then I think it hit her – whack! She felt what she'd lost, what it could have been like. She got angry with me and her tongue lashed out. After a bit she fell asleep on the settee so I was angry, and sad. I went into the bedroom and left her there. Left her nightshirt and the duvet over the chair, left the light on and went to bed.

I've never really recovered from Sheila but in retrospect I'm glad we didn't stay together. I've always admired couples that have been together for life – Jan and Bert in Blackburn, the two I met in the police, Miss Ellis and her friend – but I've come to realise that's not who I am. I'm a free spirit. If Sheila and I hadn't parted we'd have become Darby and Joan. I wouldn't have liked that.

23

A Repertoire of Lovely Sounds

I worked at the handicapped school for over ten years – through all the difficult times with Sheila. I loved those children and I'm still good friends with one boy who turned out to be gay. He and his boyfriend have been very good to me. He comes now to do odd-jobs for me. He likes to call me 'Old bag' which makes me laugh.

The next ten years were to be happy years but there was always something missing. I'd got the love of my sister and her children – as much as I wanted – showered with it. But there was that little bit missing. If there could have been a woman around, it would have been perfection. Without a woman in my life, I devoted myself in other directions.

When I was reaching retirement age, a social worker I knew through the school said he'd got a nice little job for me if I'd like it. There was a family with a handicapped boy who was having to be expelled from another school for disabled children. His name was Keith and he'd started making noises. It was just like a cow in labour – really loud and piercing. The school couldn't cope with it any longer. Keith was fourteen and because of the law he had to have at least two hours tuition under the Education Act, he had to be taught even if he was very handicapped.

So I said, "Yes, suit me fine. Providing we hit it off – very important." He said, "Oh, I think you will but the parents are very jealous about him – he's the world to them."

We went to see this child – he looked like a child, sitting up in a big cot. Now, it might sound a bit inhuman but I didn't know what he was going to do so I approached him like you go to an animal you don't know or a dog that might bite you. I went very cautiously, cooing and whispering and looking straight in his eye.

"Now Keith, I'm going to come and look after you. We're going to have lots of fun."

He looked at his mum and dad and they were looking very severe. I said a few more words and his face broke into smiles. And you could hear the mother and father almost go "Ahhh" with relief. I went up and touched him, got hold of his hands and the social worker asked them if they would take me on trial? Oh yes, they'd take me.

Instantly I saw the other side of this disabled boy. Mentally he was only perhaps eighteen months old but he was normal size, not as tall as me, and slender. His gums were awful because of all the drugs he'd taken from birth and his teeth were like baby teeth but I thought he was a lovely kid. He'd got the most fantastically beautiful eyes.

I found that Keith liked red so when I went to see him I always wore something red. I thought up all sorts of activities for him. I was filled with ideas because I'd been at the handicapped school and I'd learnt a lot of handicraft for children. I made a big box with different textures on every side and a hole he could put his hand in and feel fur inside or perhaps pull something out. I made him no end of things.

They taught me about his needs. He always had the same thing for breakfast – those mattresses – Weetabix. He loved his Weetabix, two or three every morning with a pint of milk and his pills. The pills had to go on the first spoonful before he could properly taste. He had epilepsy and would sometimes just make a noise and go off in a fit. They told me exactly what to do and they showed me how to change him, to put nappies on because he was doubly incontinent. The mother was thrilled because she was able to go out shopping after a little while, when she trusted me.

Keith was a joy to be with, a bundle of love. There was no aggression in him, no anger. I only saw him once in tears – when he was having teeth trouble and we took him to the children's hospital. All the little tiny tots around and there was this big boy climbing on his mother's knee because he was in such pain.

If he didn't like you doing something and he wanted to say no, he just put his hand up on your chest and gently pushed you away, with the gentlest of movements. He couldn't speak but he had a repertoire of lovely sounds that all meant something. You'd read books to him and he'd look at them – I don't think he'd understand anything, he'd just copy you. He'd get hold of a book and it'd be upside down and he'd be going, "Ee-oh-aah-aah." And I'd whisper, "There's a clever boy, there's a good boy."

At that time he couldn't walk but he could go on his bottom and move about. Mother and I made him a pair of special walking shoes like snowshoes for two pairs of feet. We put Keith's feet in and my feet went behind his. When I bent my knee he'd got to bend his knee. We'd go round like this, laughing and making fun but he couldn't do it. One leg seemed a little bit out of position, so they sent a physiotherapist who decided he'd got a dislocated hip. That was why he'd been yelling all that time, making those awful noises. The poor little thing, couldn't tell anybody where it was hurting and there we were, trying to make him walk.

When I reached the age of sixty-five I got a letter that the council sent to everybody reaching retirement age – sorry, your employment is terminated, blah-blah-blah. The parents went mad. They said, "They can't stop you coming. How can we tell our son that his nurse-teacher can't come any more because she's too old? It'd break his heart." I said, "Nothing is stopping me coming to this boy. He's part of me now." The father canvassed the Education Department and Social Services and in the end they decided Keith must have somebody for as long as he was alive so they created a special post for me. They thought he would die quite soon but he defied them all. He wasn't going to die, he was having too good a time on earth.

I learnt a lot from that family about patience and not seeing anything that other people might think was a bit repulsive. My friend, Tonks, came to see me once and asked to go to Keith. As we're coming out she says, "Yes, he has beautiful eyes." I said, "Don't you think he looks like other children?" She says, "Oh no, definitely not." To me he looked like other children by then. I used to take him out in his pushchair, wheel him down to the beach. The lifeguards would either take his chair down or carry him down and sit him on the pebbles. He loved going round on the pebbles and playing with them. Other children would come over. Sometimes mothers would snatch them away and I'd say, "He's perfectly harmless, he won't hurt your children."

He loved flowers. If I took him out and there was something hanging over somebody's garden, he'd have it – put his hand out and pull it down. So he'd be sitting in his chair with a piece of green twig or a flower. After a long, long time people began to get more educated to this type of person. If you kept to the same route and went to the same places you'd find people began to speak to you: "Can I look after him for you? Shall I stay with him for a little while? Do you want to go to the lavatory or anything?" Going down George Street in Hove, the main shopping street, the shopkeepers all knew him. If he could grab a cucumber he'd love it. You'd take it off him and they'd say, "Let him have it." People wanted to be nice to you but they were embarrassed.

He'd play with his toys for hours. He had a bunch of coloured strings like a ball of knitting, all jumbled up. He'd hold it up to the light and look through it. I'm sure he used to see things we didn't see. One day when we were out looking round a junk shop on one of our walks he found a draining mat that you put in the sink, a little plastic pad with square holes in: "Ee-oo-aahh" – look what I've got. It became one of his favourite toys. He would flick it, he'd bend it and let it spring back, he'd put it up to the light and look through it. He loved it.

Keith and Barbara.

•

His sounds got more and more varied with the stimulation but when he was poorly he wouldn't make any sounds. He went into hospital with a temperature nearly dying one time and the doctor said, "This boy is almost in a coma now. If you leave him he's just going to quietly die. Don't you think that would be the best thing for him?" Dad said, "Don't you dare let my boy die! Don't you dare." Keith was in hospital quite a few weeks then and he got a private room of his own. The nurses hadn't a clue what to do. "Pill time! Here's your medicine!" He didn't know what they meant, he spat the pills out. They didn't know how to change him, a boy that was fully matured with a little eighteen-month mind. They didn't know what to do – try and fix a thing on his winkle, a baggy here and a something there. He didn't want it, he didn't understand it – they didn't understand him. So we always had to have someone there – and you'd show the staff how to put his nappies on, how to give him his medicine, take the Weetabix with you. They were grateful to you for showing them.

This kid and I adored each other in the end. We were in love, both of us. If I went on holiday I'd tell him, "Now I'm not going to come for a little while. As soon as I come back I will come and see you. You be a good boy whilst I'm away." When I came back, cold shoulder and a little sulky mouth. I'd say that I was sorry and I did love him. And I'd try and put my arm round him but he'd turn away. Took about three or four minutes before his hand went up – his favourite was to put one arm round your neck and pull you down onto the bed and hold you so tight you thought you were going to choke. He was very strong. And he'd hold you there like that and grin the face over – "I've got you now, don't you dare go away again."

I think it was because he was so helpless that I really loved him. I was very important to him. He took the place of a son for me. After Sheila and I finally parted, my love had to go somewhere and I heaped it all on Keith. I was with him eighteen years.

Christmas morning 1993 the family were upstairs having their Christmas dinner. They had cameras in Keith's bedroom so they could keep looking and see he was all right. If he made a noise they could hear him and speak down to him. On this occasion they'd settled him, he'd had his dinner, was playing with something. Then one of them said, "Oh, look at Keith, he looks a bit funny." They rushed down the stairs, Dad first, like lightning. Keith was going blue in the face, not like his usual fit. Dad immediately started resuscitation and yelled for them to send for an ambulance. The ambulance crew came with their cylinder and they tried to resuscitate him.

He was in a coma. They took him to hospital. They didn't know what it was, it was something he hadn't had before so they just put him in for observation. There were always two people at his bed –

I did my stint in the mornings – but he never regained consciousness.

They'd had someone come from London from the organ bank and the parents said, "Anything he's got that can go to anybody, please, it's to be used." So the hospital was prepared. Blow me, when it was clear he was going to be dying any minute, they hadn't got a pathologist there so nobody could operate to take out his organs. But Keith waited till the morning when the doctor came back on duty before he died. Dad was so proud when they wrote to say that two young men had had their sight restored with Keith's corneas and another young man had been given one of his heart valves.

I still miss Keith. All right, his brain might have been incomplete and damaged but there was something there in its place. You'd only need to look at that boy to feel a warmth – you'd only need to look at his eyes and you felt brilliant. It was uncanny. I have the feeling that these kind of people have got an extra sense that we've lost. We're cluttered with so much civilisation and so many modern things that it's crowded out the natural naiveties. And the sweetnesses of life are crushed.

Barbara, 1989.

•

24

A Horrible Illness

I'm not a political animal. When the Sussex Gay Liberation Front started up in Brighton in the early seventies I thought, good luck to them, let them get on with it. But when Aids reared its ugly head I felt I must do something to help – it could have struck the lesbian girls, not the gay boys.

The Sussex Aids Centre and Helpline was started in 1985. It was just called the Aids Helpline then and I was in it practically from the beginning. It was in the press, asking for volunteers. I phoned and it was Graham Wilkinson who answered – he was one of the founders of it. There were only a few of them running it then. I was asked if I'd had any training. I said, "Well I'm old, I'm seventy, there's not much I don't know and I've got common sense. Surely there's something I can do? I'll scrub floors, anything to help." I was told I really had to have training and the next training course was in January. I said, "Well put me down for the course but I've got to do something, I'm desperate to help. Take my phone number." A few days later he rang me up and said, "Did you really mean you'd scrub floors?" I said, "Yes." He said, "Well, it isn't scrubbing floors but it's helping in the kitchen so you won't see much of the client."

"I'll do it."

The first time I went, the door opened and there was this young fella in his pyjamas and I thought it was the lover. I didn't think it was the fella that was ill because he looked so perky and he was so friendly and pleased to see me. He was trying out some special diet. Everything had to be thoroughly disinfected – permanganate of potash in the water you washed the vegetables in and a special machine for squeezing liver and fruit juices. Awful things he had to eat and drink because they thought it would help. I had to be in the kitchen to prepare all this and to wash up because everything had to be washed and then boiling water poured on it. What a palaver!

I used to take the laundry to a launderette because we had a lot of washing and occasionally a bit of ironing. And then I would go to the health-food store and get all the special things he wanted. Another time I had to go down to the photocopy shop because he was writing some papers that he thought would help others after-wards, after he died. There were little jobs he wanted doing like mending a lamp that had been wobbly for years. I'd traipse it off to some helpful gay boys and they'd gladly repair it.

Then he became really ill. I didn't see him then. The mother came and she stayed in a little bed and breakfast place two doors away. I was only picking up the laundry and taking it back to the door, I didn't even go in. One day it struck me that the mother was having a bad time of it so I asked her if she would like to come and have a cup of tea with me. She would come and she would weep and she'd tell me about when he was a little boy, anything, talking about her son.

There was another fella in Hove. I got very, very fond of him. He was in his seventies and nobody believed he had Aids at his age. I was in charge of a team. Somebody went in the mornings to set his pills out for him. Somebody went in at midday to make sure he'd had his food and, as he got worse, to wash him, change his bed. And then in the evening somebody would go in again. It got to the pitch where we had to leave messages for each other on a big pad – what we had done and what we'd changed and what food and pills we'd given him.

He was a very, very sick man in the end. His skin was flaking all the time and I used to get the dustpan and brush to sweep it off the sheets. He was in agony, that man. He died in hospital but only just got there before he died. It was very sad. It's all very sad.

After that I got very close to a young fella called Barry. I was even washing him when the nurse couldn't come. He had Kaposi's sarcoma – black marks under his skin – it's a kind of cancer. He made me very humble. I used to feel, why have I been given this task? To wash this sick man and to love this sick man? Because he didn't look nice by then – these black marks on his nose, on his cheek, on his body – it's a horrible thing to look at, and painful. I used to think I was washing Jesus's feet. It was a most peculiar feeling.

I broke my heart when he died, just yelled and yelled. Then when I'd been through about six or seven, or eight, to the ninth and tenth funeral, I stopped weeping. I thought, why am I crying? I'm only crying for myself. Now I don't cry, or I do cry but I don't break my heart. I'm relieved because they're out of their pain, they're out of their waiting. You just give thanks – in my case that I've known them – and you give thanks for their life. My life has been enriched no end by the relationships I've made with people that I've visited. I loved the work because they taught me a lot. It doesn't matter how old you are, you're still learning. It does make you realise how bloody well off you are, not to be having something like that. Because it's a horrible illness. Cancer's bad enough but this is a pernicious horrible thing.

I've been to some wonderful funerals. Two of my boys even told me what they wanted me to wear.

"Now don't wear that hat you wore for so-and-so will you? I want you to wear that red hat. Now which coat you going to wear?"

"Well, shall I wear my little grey one or my black...?"

"No, wear your grey one. No, I don't want you in grey, I don't want you in black. Haven't you got a white coat? Well, you'll have to buy a white coat won't you? I want you in a white coat."

25

Locked in a Fierce Embrace

My favourite of all the people I buddied was Ann-Marie. I met her at a women's party. We'd finished eating and were sitting on the floor round the fire. There was a knock at the door and this vision came in. She'd got a very old, black, faded straw hat covered in artificial flowers, high boots and a little short skirt which just covered her bum. She walked in and she said, "I'm Ann-Marie and I'm HIV positive." I thought, well, what an introduction! Nobody else there was HIV positive, nobody. I thought, what a brave thing to say!

I said, "You're the most beautiful woman I've seen in many a year. Sit here, next to me, there's a space on the floor." She said, "Oh, thank you." We chatted and I couldn't take my eyes off this girl. I left early, because they were then passing round a bit of cannabis and I said I'd had my time of that. I didn't hear anything of her for about two months and then she went to the helpline and asked for me. And so I came to look after her. She wasn't ill at that point, she was all right, full of energy, loved doing anything, loved shopping.

If she wanted to go to a club she'd ring me up because she wanted an escort, she wanted to feel safe. She'd been turned out of a straight club. The bouncer came up to her and said, "I'm sorry but somebody has asked will I tell you to leave please." She said, "Why?"

"Because they said you've got Aids and I have to."

They actually turned her out so after that she'd go to any of the gay boys' clubs and they let her in.

By this time I'd moved to Kemptown, to a little flat near the

Ann-Marie.

•

seafront – the big Regency terraces that Brighton's famous for. I'd been told Kemptown was where all the gay boys lived – the Mecca for homosexuals. And that they all walked up and down St James's Street with handbags – which wasn't true – and earrings – which wasn't true. It was an arty-crafty area of Brighton, had a bit of fire with it. It wasn't like the suburbs. It was a place for gay men, that was partly why I moved there – even though they were boys they were my own lot, as it were. They would understand and I'd feel at home. Nobody said I'd find lesbians there. Lesbians have never colonised any particular place in Brighton – they're dotted about all over and they always have been.

Ann-Marie was very beautiful, lovely-natured girl. Everybody in Kemptown and all round about knew Ann-Marie because she was spectacular. She would wear the most outrageous clothes and get away with them. She bought a lot from the BBC when they were selling up some theatrical things. One of the special outfits was a Spanish top with leather trousers underneath. Or another beautiful thing was leggings with laces at the side right to the top. You could see a slice of leg all the way up, then she'd have a little short top on. She had a very big black hat, it must have been three feet across and loads of bracelets jangling around. She walked with her head high and her bottom sticking out. Her make-up was very white and eyes very made up with a sequin stuck somewhere on her face and a ring in her nose.

She was with her boyfriend. She called herself bisexual – she'd got girlfriends and boyfriends. So she was with Ben. I took them for a run in the country once with Mrs Crabtree, my friend from teaching. We took a flask and some buns, it wasn't a summer's day. We went down to Piddinghoe village and there was a magnolia tree with some branches hanging over into the lane.

"Oh," said Ann-Marie, "please stop and let me look at them because I think they have a lovely smell."

So she wriggled through the window and she plucked off some branches of these magnolias. Mrs Crabtree was horrified. She said, "You shouldn't take those, they belong to the lady with the garden." And Ben said, "It's leaning over in the lane so it belongs to anybody who's passing. Anyway all trees belong to God." On we went, wandering down this lane and there was a tree that had been struck by lightning. We had our picnic there and after a few minutes, "Where's Ben? Ben? Ben?" Then we heard a muffled voice saying, "You don't know what I've found, there's a big hole in this tree and I've got in it." That's how they were, just like two children on that picnic, they just loved it.

Ann-Marie and Mrs Crabtree were having a deep conversation about death, about funerals. They were both saying they weren't afraid to die and they both knew they were going to die pretty soon. Afterwards Mrs Crabtree said how much she'd enjoyed the conversation and what a lot she'd learned from this plucky girl, as she called her. She was a very brave girl, she knew she was going to die, she knew she had Aids but she really had come to terms with it. Amongst their own circle of friends I know at least two women who were told they had HIV and were nearly going berserk. Ann-Marie spent such a long time with them, she was counselling them and she really helped them. She was comforting, she'd just got a knack of saying the right things.

As for counselling her, I think she counselled me. I told her about my mastectomy and how I'd felt so bad about myself. She said, "I want to see it." I'd never shown anybody. I said, "Oh, it's just a pucker of a scar. You don't want to see anything as ugly as that." She said, "I want to see it," in her very quiet, determined voice – she never spoke loud. So she saw it and she just bent down and started kissing it, saying how beautiful it was, to make me feel better about it. She was such a wise little creature and so courageous.

She'd come and knock at my door at six o'clock in the morning and say, "It's Ann-Marie, can I have a little sleep? Shall we have our breakfast together? I'm ever so hungry." So sometimes she'd lie on the couch and have a couple of hours' sleep and we'd have breakfast together and then she'd go home back to Ben. She loved coming for supper and we'd have candlelight and best tablecloth on and cutlery and she behaved like a little lady. One time Ben rang the doorbell and I said, "No, I'm sorry, you can't come in, we're having girly talk."

I knew I was falling in love with her and I thought, you cannot do this, you're here to help this girl, you're here as a volunteer worker. And you're far too old anyway to be making love to this young creature. But she did everything to get me to make love to her. It was a strain on me because I'm only human. It was very difficult.

I remember we went into Hanningtons department store and she said, "Oh, do you think I would look lovely in these tiger tights? I'm going to buy some next week and I'll dress up for you," with a meaningful look. I said, "Well, as long as you don't behave like a tiger." She said, "You'll have to wait and find out." I said, "I must go now, I have this other appointment, I'll come to the door with you." In the doorway, she snatched me, pressed herself up against me, pressed me up against the door, this little thing. I had to put my arms around her, I would have toppled over. Arms round each other, locked in a fierce embrace and she was kissing me like mad and saying, "Oh don't leave me! Don't leave me! Can't you stay with me a little bit longer?" People were swinging through the door and looking at us. I thought they were going to arrest us. No shame whatsoever! Finally she let me go and off I went. But that was nothing strange for her. Very passionate.

She would try all sorts of tricks to get me to make love to her. Sometimes I'd go in and she would be walking round with just her tights on and then she'd say, "Oh, I must change these tights and put some others on." She thought nothing of walking about naked and climbing about, this beautiful creature with long black hair, looking like a nymph. I gave her some sexy red and black underwear that I'd kept for years and years, that I used to wear for Sheila. She devoured it. She put it on there and then. Swanking round the place. Little bitch.

She'd say, "Can I show you a trick that I used to do in Amsterdam?" She'd crouch down on the floor onto a piece of folded paper and clutch the paper and make it open and shut. She said, "This is called the Butterfly Dance!"

Later on she said, "Why don't you make love to me? It means nothing to me that you're an older person and I do love you." I think she thought that if we were lovers everyone would think, how strange and how wonderful. It appealed to her as a romance. I tried to say, "Well, if we do have a deep relationship and you die, I'm going to be bereft and if I die, what are you going to feel like? You'll be bereft." It was difficult and I was tempted. I think it's the strictest discipline that I've ever had to take. Every time I pass Hanningtons doorway now, I think, oooh! A gasp, a gasp of delight.

She died suddenly. I always went up on Sunday evenings, always without fail. And I would usually take a bit of something nice for us to eat together because Sunday was their zero day. On this occasion I was running late and Ben came to my door and said, "Ann-Marie's dead." That was all. I said, "What do you mean, Ben?" Then he told me the story. She'd felt ill in the night and said, "Oh, I'm too hot." She did have terrible sweats. She'd said, "I'll have to lie in the hall and I'll take the beanbags." She was always doing that, feeling hot and throwing half her clothes off. When he got up she was lying on the beanbags with hardly any cover over her. He'd covered her over with a coat and gone out for a walk, gone off to see his pals. When he came back she still hadn't moved, so he thought, well, she'll be cross if she's missing all the Sunday, I'd better wake her up. He leaned over to kiss her and found she was cold. He got her onto the bed, brushed her hair, put her some make-up on and then he came to tell me.

I said, "We'll have to call the police, Ben." He said, "No. I'm coming to you because I knew you wouldn't inform the police." They'd had a pact between them that if one died, the other would sleep with them all night in the same bed, sleep next to them. I said, "You can't do it, Ben. You know it's just not allowed. If you hadn't come to me and you'd done it on your own, nobody would have known but you've told me and I've got to do something about it." I said, "Look, if Father Marcus at Open Door says we've to have the police, will you have the police?"

"Oh, Father Marcus won't say that."

"Well, if he says, will you go?"

So we knocked at his door and the window was open upstairs and I shouted, "It's Barbara." He ran down in his dressing gown. And I told him. He put his arms round me. That was all. Then round Ben. And we just stood quiet there. And then he said, "Ben, we'll have to go, we'll go to your flat, we'll have to inform the police."

"They'll take her away and they'll question me."

He said, "No, what have you to fear, Ben?"

We were positive, we were both positive that Ben knew nothing about this. Her drugs for the evening were still there so she hadn't taken an overdose.

About three months before that she had begun to be a bit funny with me. She wouldn't let me in the flat when I'd gone and rung the bell. She'd say, "I don't want to see you." And when I did see her, she'd say, "Do you think I'm losing my looks? Do you think I'm still beautiful? Do you think my face is getting thin? Is my body as lovely as it's always been?" She'd told me, "I never want to look ill. I hope I shall die quickly." I think she realised she was losing her looks, losing her memory. She thought, I'm not going to go through all that. I've seen it. I'm going to end it. And I think she just shut her eyes and willed herself to die. I was sorry because I would have liked to have been there and she knows she could have done it with me there. She could have told me, "I want to die tonight." She knew I would have taken that but no, she did it all on her own, not even in bed with Ben.

It was a big shock and Marcus was just a wonderful friend. We left him there to deal with everything and I took Ben back home and he stayed a week. We had two beds in the bedroom and all that week he was calling out, "Are you all right? Are you all right? I'm here, I'm looking after you."

"Yes, Ben, I'm all right, I'm looking after you."

And then we'd hold hands across the gap between the beds. We really needed each other, to comfort each other because nobody else understood. We both loved her.

I was asked to go to the funeral but I couldn't take it. It was in Liverpool. I just sent a red rose. But some months later we had a thanksgiving service in St Nicholas church and quite a lot of people came.

She was a little devil sometimes but she did have a very, very kind streak. People were stopping us in St James's Street that week when she died and saying, "Oh, I've heard about Ann-Marie, I'm ever so sorry."

So we had a lovely service and her parents came to my flat the last evening. We just talked Ann-Marie the whole night until our eyelids were drooping and our mouths were dry. They were telling me about when she was a girl and what a trouble she was and such an anxiety to them. And how she first started to take drugs and how upset they all were. She and Ben both contracted HIV through their drug abuse, dirty needles. Very sad.

So then I took Ben under my wing. I spoilt him rotten and he spoilt me rotten and called me Mumsie. Sometimes he'd say, "Oh, I do miss Ann-Marie," and sometimes we'd just talk Ann-Marie talk and laugh at the silly things she used to do. He'd mimic her walking round the room with her little bottom sticking out. He'd talk to Ann-Marie when he was alone: he hallucinated a bit. He was a sweet man.

So that's the story of Ann-Marie, my little Ann-Marie. My sweet little poppet. She gave me a good few laughs. It was a big blow to me because I loved that girl. She was about thirty-two, I think. She died at Easter 1991 and some time later Ben died too. I stopped Aids work then.

26

A Blessed Life

I keep young now, I think, because I do things. I don't think of getting old. I'm horrified when I think how old I really am. I have a wonderful social life. I visit people. People visit me. I go out walking over the Downs with the local lesbian walking group. My ex-lovers come to see me or I go to see them. Most of the people that I've loved, I'm still in contact with them. It's lovely, there's a warmth when we meet. I like to sit back and reminisce. I don't want to go round clubs now but I love dancing. I'm turned on when I hear some good music, or drums.

I've met some wonderful people all through my life. All along the way I've made good friends, very constant friends and treasured them as friends. In that respect I've been very fortunate. They've been a great help to me when I've had my ups and downs – when I've been in trouble or down in the depths or a relationship has come to an end. When I've thought it was the end of the world, they've helped me and got me through.

I make friends easily. I love to have a good gossip with someone. In the police I was used to interrogating people and wanting to know all about them. I love people and I like to help them. If I'm shy I manage to conceal it until I know someone a bit better. It must be terrible if you're so closed up and shy you can't stretch out to somebody when you want to. It's been easy for me. I'm open to receiving.

I think I've had and am having a wonderful life. I suppose some people go through life without achieving one ambition. So I'm lucky I achieved a few. I was very fortunate in having Trudi, a beautiful young girl, to have my first love affair with and to have my first

Barbara (second from left) with members of Brighton Women's Walking Group, Rottingdean.

•

home with Madeleine, another beautiful woman of character. I've a lot to be thankful for.

I've always been blessed, always. I've always been very loved, all my life, by my parents and family and friends. My sister, Midge, has never been far away. I've always been accepted by her and her two sons. Now I have the joy of three beautiful great-nieces. I'm lucky to have a family I can share. They all look out for me.

Every morning now, when I wake up, I thank God for another new day. I haven't been a devout active Christian. I try to live my life as well as I can and that's my way of worship. I've never thought that God would disapprove of me being a lesbian. If it's love, if it's true love, that's all God cares about.

It might seem in my seventy years as a lesbian that I've been a bit promiscuous but I don't think on the whole I was. They all meant something to me, every woman that I took to bed. I didn't really run amok. I didn't go round with my tongue hanging out – "Oh, I must find somebody for tonight," – I was never that desperate. All the girlfriends I had, I still loved them when we parted. There was never bad blood, or if there was it was always made up at some later date. And if it was me that was wrong, I admitted I had done the wrong thing or been a bit rotten. Nobody's a paragon. I've hurt people along the road. But when you're young you do those things. You think of yourself too much, I suppose, if you're in love.

But I have to say that anyone who's just realised they're a lesbian and thinks, Oh God, it's going to be an awful life – it isn't. It's wonderful because if you wait long enough you find the right person. And if it's not the right person, okay, you've had a go and it didn't work – find somebody else. But never, never spin it out. Say goodbye. Say, "Go, darling, go. You can be friends with me. I'll be here." You may be breaking your heart but if you really love them, you'll let them go. However much it hurts. There's nothing worse than letting something die slowly. You have to be heartbroken, it's part of it.

I don't know that I want to be tied now with a partner because I'm too selfish. I've got my own way of living and my own way of going out and coming in and it would interrupt my peaceful life. I'm not saying that I don't fancy girls I meet – I'm not immune, even at my age. A few years ago, when they had communal changing rooms in the boutiques, I found it a bit of a strain. I'd be trying a garment on and they'd be running round in their little panties and little bras and I'd think, Oh! God, take your eyes off, look the other way, just try on what you're trying on. I'm clever now at keeping it in check.

Sometimes I'm walking along the street and I see a lovely girl all beautifully turned out and I just go up to her and say, "Oh, excuse me, I do think you look so lovely with the way you're dressed and the way you look, you don't mind me telling you, do you?" And they say, "No, no, thank you." My sister says I'll get my face slapped one day.

Not so many years ago, I saw a beautiful woman on the Underground, there were only two of us left in the carriage as we were approaching my stop. I crossed over to her and I said, "I'm sorry, don't think I'm rude but before I get off the train, I must tell you you're so beautiful I can't stop gazing at you." She giggled and smiled and I said, "I'm getting off here, where are you getting off?" She said, "Wim-bla-don." I said, "Oh, I'll come to Wim-bla-don then." And she said, "Oh yes, yes!" Sat next to her and asked her a question or two. She hardly spoke any English. Then I said, "Would you like me to see you to your flat?"

"Oh yes, yes."

I didn't have much time that day because I was supposed to be getting back somewhere but I was just swept off my feet – she looked so lovely. She said, "Will you have some tea?" I said, "Oh yes, I like teatime." We had a cuddle and a little fondling and a little love on the couch. Very nice. So after that she was phoning me up and saying, "Will you come for teatime?" I went several times before she had to go back home, it was lovely.

I've still got it in me. I'm still on the lookout. I can't be celibate for ever. It's not in my nature. We'll see. As we used to say in Blackburn, "If it's to be, it'll be."

Index

Bell, Barbara (*cont.*)
the beach in Ireland, 67; giving
the glad eye on the street, 74;
stockings and suspenders, 75;
asked to put on a lesbian sex
show, 75–6; freedom of choice in
London, 89; wriggling on the
bus, 89; flirting with ATS girls,
90; butch and fem, 41–3, 66–7,
72–5, 91, 138; whipping, 91–2;
passing on a new trick, 92;
dildoes, 92; magnolias, 92; oral
sex, 92–3; bosoms, 114–5, 158;
paying for sex, 120; women in
glasses, 122; seducing with
gramophone records, 123–4; sex
with straight women, 125–6; in
Sheila's car, 140; in the open air,
155; effect of mastectomy, 160;
passionate letters, 163–4;
overtures from Ann-Marie,
182–3; still on the look-out
188–9;
work: dairy, 32; photographic
modelling, 43–4; Woolworths,
44; police, 57–9, 60–65, 72,
75–6, 77–83, *84*, 97–8, 102;
war effort, 87; mannequin,
98–100, *99*, 102; teaching, 107;
teaching housecraft in Shepherd's
Bush, 113; deputy headmistress
at Delrow House, 113–15;
teaching at Staines, 115–16, 121;
teaching at Lewes, 124, 127;
teaching in Nigeria, 132–5;
teaching handicapped children in
Brighton, 144, 153, 167;
nurse-teacher to Keith, 167–73,
171; buddying, 175–85;
World War Two, 62, *63*, 70,

Bell, Barbara (*cont.*)
77–83, *78*, 85–8, 94;
Bell, Beatrice (Barbara's mother), 11,
12, *13*, 15, 16, 18–19, 20, 23, 29,
30–31, 37, 42, 43, 46, 53, 54, 56,
57, 58, 59, 88, 94–6, *95*, 102–4
Bell, Joe (Barbara's father), 11, 12,
13, *13*, 15–16, 20, 23–5, 29–30,
33, 42, 53, 55, 57–8, 59, 70, 94,
96–7
Bell, Marjorie (Midge, Barbara's
sister), 12, *13*, 25, 30, 38, 47, 94,
96, 98, 105–7, *106*, 108–110,
113, 116, 128, 142, 151–3, *152*,
160, 187, 189
Bell, Stanley (Barbara's brother), 12,
13, 48, *82*, 83
Ben, 180, 181, 183–5
Brighton Women's Walking Group,
186, *187*

Carbone, Emanuelo, 111–12,
116–19, 158
Carbone, 'Mami', 116, 119, 127–8
Carbone, Syria, 118–9, *155*
Chapman, Diana, 144–5
Christian Endeavour Friendship
Movement, 33
cinema, 37, 53, 90
Crabtree, Mrs, 142, 151, 180, 181
Cyril, 36–7, 38, 39, 45, 49, 53, 56,
57, 85, 100, 126

Dent, Miss, 26, 27–8, 58

Ellis, Miss, 146–7, 165, *165*, 166
Emma, 153–6, *155*
'Experiment' (Cole Porter), 38–9

Florrie, 32, 49, 53